A NEW CONCISE REFERENCE DICTIONARY AND GLOSSARY OF USAGE TERMS AND SUBJECTS IN CONTEMPORARY ART

Neal Brown

Sorika

Published in 2014 by Sorika

Published by arrangement with
ArtReview magazine

Design
Helios Capdevila

Printing
GGP Media GmbH
Pößneck, Germany

The publisher wishes to thank Richard Greer for his generous support of this publication.

ISBN 978-0-9575573-3-8

Edition of 1500 copies

Frontispiece:
Elliott Erwitt, Venice, 1965
Magnum Photos

About The Author

Neal Brown is the author of *Meditations on Art Hate* (L-13, 2010), *Tracey Emin* (Tate Publishing, 2006), *Mat Collishaw* (Other Criteria, 2006), and *Billy Childish: A Short Study* (L-13, 2008). As well as writing for *ArtReview*, he has written about art for *Flash Art*, *Frieze*, *Art Monthly*, *Modern Painters*, *Parkett*, *Art and Christianity*, *Tate Etc.*, and the *Independent on Sunday*. He is the author of numerous catalogue essays for artists, is editor and publisher of *Nineteen Raptures* (NB Publishing, 2009), and curated *To the Glory of God: New Religious Art* at the second Liverpool Biennial.

For further information please see *www.nealbrown.net*

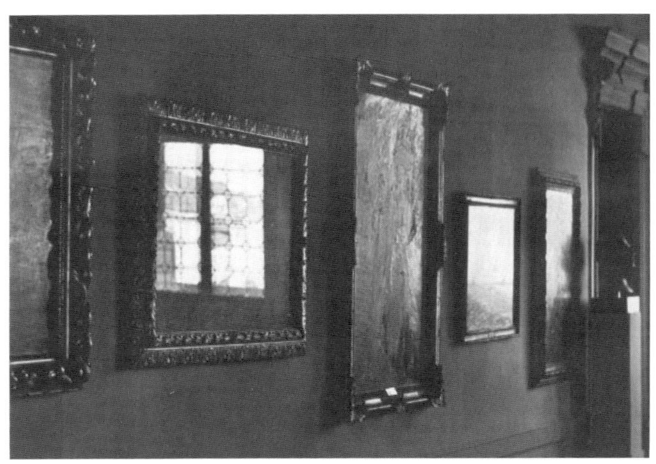

This book is gratefully and respectfully dedicated to the editors for who or whom I have written about art. See → Hugh **Allan**, Lewis **Biggs**, Jessamy **Calkin**, David **Chandler**, Suzanne **Cotter**, Gemma **de Cruz**, Michael **Curran**, Celia **Davies**, Charlotte **Edwards**, Marcus **Field**, Rebecca **Fortey**, Simon **Grant**, Louise **Gray**, Elaine **Hake**, Jennifer **Higgie**, Antonia **Hodgson**, David **Jenkins**, Kira **Jolliffe**, Ray **Jones** and **Rodent**, Florian **Kobler**, Holly **Kyte**, Mark **Law**, Susan **Lawson**, Steve **Lowe**, Honey **Luard**, Zoë **Manzi**, Christiane **Meyer-Stoll**, Laura **Moffatt**, Charlotte **Mullins**, Harry **Pye**, Cay Sophie **Rabinowitz**, Jane **Rankin-Reid**, Mark **Rappolt**, Mary **Richards**, Michele **Robecchi**, James **Roberts**, Linda **Saunders**, Matthew **Slotover**, Polly **Staple**, David **Terrien**, Michael **VerMeulen**, Ossian **Ward**, Nicolas **Wegner**, Tim **Willis**, Andrew **Wilson**, Karen **Wright**.

Contents

Foreword by Matthew Collings

My immediate associations when I think of the concept of Neal's book are a) the appendix to Gustave Flaubert's *Bouvard and Pécuchet* (1881), and b) artists Fischli/Weiss. The former is full of hilarious drollisms, in which a thing is 'always' connected to another thing and you know it means you must never forget in conversation to name or utter the sound of these two things in the same breath (but not necessarily have the faintest idea why, or even what one or both of them is, or means). With the latter, the Swiss postmodernists, the important thing is a collection of clay sculptures from 1981, named *Suddenly This Overview*, each possessing an individual title that, in an artworld context, could easily suggest a certain received-idea mentality – an example would be, say, *Difference and Repetition.* Fischli/Weiss created a sculpture with this title, as part of the *Suddenly This Overview* series, and of course it's a book by Gilles Deleuze. There was a time when it was important in order to make it clear to readers that you were not an art writer to be fucked with, to mention 'rhizomes' once or twice. Then it became absolutely not the thing to do and if you went out on a limb and did it anyway it would be considered pitiable. In Fischli/Weiss's series, very bluntly modelled real-world objects, from people to potatoes, fire to cars, turn out to be inescapably clear 3-D signs for concepts that, in the land of the art intelligentsia, should always have infinite indeterminacy, so that whoever deploys them has infinite power. *Difference and Repetition* for example is rendered as two innocently grinning identical provincial idiots. And yet the success of this group of works is not just due to a comic cutting down to size or literal embodiment of complex metaphors, metaphors whose usage in a certain social context is considered a sign of complex mental ability. That level of fun is certainly there. But what has happened beyond that is that something new has arrived: genuine complexity. Not an anti-intellectual door-closing statement that withers anyone's natural eagerness to try out an idea or two. But rather a real game of new ideas or flight paths (here I use the long since discredited Deleuze and Guattarian fave term.) As Albion is always yoked to perfidious and to white, not to mention Napoleon ('came jolly close to conquering it') in *Bouvard and Pécuchet*, and art leads to the poorhouse – 'What's the use of it, since we're replacing it with machines that do better and work faster?' – so certain nutty stuff must always happen in the professional world of superb hustlers Neal works in, even though, as he is aware, it's completely arbitrary and will soon be out of fashion. But in deliberately foolishly monumentalising, or solidifying, a fugitive brilliance as he does in entry after entry in his funny index of art ideas, which is really a map of thought gone incredibly wrong, he might be creating a third power. Neither rhetorical career-conscious bullshit nor a baseline of bourgeois common sense, it is his own kingdom of freedom in which he finally shrugs off stuff that has been weighing him down and repressing him for years. For the rest of us it can't be quite that, because such weighing down is always personal. But at least we can roam in this created world and genuinely feel that we've benefited from an intellectual service. The cleaners coming round and doing a genuine bit of dusting and hoovering, unclogging congested brains, doesn't just apply in Neal's book to the artworld talking to itself, but also the bourgeois spectator world not only interrogating the artworld (its fantasies about unmade beds as conceptual art) but also patting itself on the back for its insights into the complete non-requirement to talk to anybody since everything is already known 'Blue: a lovely, lovely colour, good for children to look at.' I also very much appreciate Neal's surrealism, in fact much more of the book is this than it is satire, or an attack on obvious targets. Bisexuals happening every two years is on one level a biennale, which is an event that has become absolutely explosive with problems since UK ordinary art journalists used to go to them wearing all-white and panama hats as if they were on holiday in Rhodesia, but also a weird poem. It has no meaning at all but sounds like the right kind of thing you'd want to hear, so that you might escape to another head place entirely, on one of those planes full of art people going to Venice, sticking out more enormous even than usual metaphorical big willies at each other, regarding famous artists they desperately believe are their friends – referring to them by their first names, or worse, intimate nicknames – and getting in casual mentions of the high-powered institutions that are paying for their trip and hotel. But then what were you doing on that plane at all? Which brings us to the question of the ideal readership. Who is it? What should they know? What should they be fed up about? I return to association. Funnily enough I once interviewed Fischli/Weiss, in Zurich as it happens, their dwelling place at the time. The one who died recently – Weiss – was tense, forever pacing the room, flinging the window open, going out for a break. I had no idea what they did really; I'd never seen any of the works we were discussing, only the film, *The Way Things Go*, which was all the rage on the biennale circuit in this particular year, 1987. But it wasn't this that was eating David, not my ignorance: they liked that and found it sympathetic. In fact 'sympathetic' was the word that sank in for me from that trip. We all went swimming in the lake after, naked, with Martin Kippenberger and their mutual gallerist, a woman, I forget her name now. And I said the magazine I edited, which had been hospitable to Kippenberger and his friends, was getting a new look done by a real designer, Neville Brody, no longer just me with a pair of scissors and an enlarger. And Kippenberger said what a shame, the old design was sympathetic. You can be ignorant and it's all right, or it might not even be ignorance. Or you can be cynical about specialised knowledge and at the same time struggling to gain some, and express both sentiments in the same bitter quips directed against it. (Oh yes, Gisela Capitain. A Cologne gallery: always say 'gallerist'.) Weiss was agitated in the interview because both of them, in their joint work as artists, really were trying to understand systems of knowledge by parodying the struggle to absorb such systems, so familiar and pathetic, especially when you are no longer of student age. The book you're about to read won't tell you anything helpful about art, like the ideal longed for primer providing the basic keys to a mystery. No book really does that. You have to read them all and reject them and then go back to them. Or I should say it tells you a helpful thing actually surprisingly often, if you know what to look for, that is, if you don't need to be told these things. But then in the same entry it immediately brings in something deeply unhelpful, such as the relationship of baboons to modern art of the post-war period, so you can be reassured, if you already knew, that objectivity is present, but thrilled that it needn't be the be all and end all, or even anything. At least, that would be how you'd rationalise what just happened if you were already aware that symmetry exists in both Don Judd's Minimalist sculptures and Fra Angelico's frescoes. In which case you wouldn't need to be told many of the things in the book that someone dutiful might class as 'helpful'. Like an answer to the question, what is geometry for in art? It's not a help book it's a fantasy, a fantasy formed from elements that you know very well like the baleful junk in your own mind, but someone else is having it. It's weird to be in their dream. What's it about? Is it their refusal to join in with a phantasmagoria no one realises isn't real, like those competitive career conversations on trips to international art hotspots? But a dream can be helpful, too. Is Minimalism religious because religious art is often geometric? It is if baboons are really all that frequent or important in contemporary art. Happy reading.

Introduction and Acknowledgements

This *New Concise Reference Dictionary and Glossary of Usage Terms and Subjects in Contemporary Art* first appeared in *ArtReview* magazine. It commenced with A in summer 2010, and concluded twenty-five columns later with Z in spring 2013. I am very grateful to Mark Rappolt, the editor of *ArtReview*, for fearlessly commissioning such a series, and to the magazine's highly informed readership for the kind tolerance they have shown it.

This edition brings the columns together, and revises and expands them with many additional entries – written as clearly and concisely as possible – so as to reflect the latest developments in the exciting field of contemporary art. It is to be hoped *Dictionary* will thus continue to serve as a useful resource for students, arts professionals and lovers of art alike. Its pocket-size format is designed to allow it to be a useful companion when visiting galleries and exhibitions.

My intention with *Dictionary* has always been to insult everyone equally, and with this edition I allow myself the small hope I may have succeeded. This includes myself, of course; truly a beast and monster, as editors can confirm. If you believe that you or some belief system you cherish has not been adequately insulted, please inform the publisher, who will note the correction for future editions. For more advanced offence it may be profitable to read *Dictionary* in conjunction with *Meditations on Art Hate* (L-13, 2010), my contribution to the internationally important *Art Hate* project originated by Billy Childish, BAR, and the L-13 Light Industrial Workshop. Extended sections of *Meditations* were published in *ArtReview* during the same period as *Dictionary*.

As well as Mark Rappolt, thanks are due to everyone at *ArtReview* – most especially to the very kind David Terrien; I would like to thank Matthew Collings for his great generosity in contributing a much appreciated foreword; Gareth McConnell at Sorika for bringing together and publishing *Dictionary* in its entirety, and for his interest and support while doing so; Helios Capdevila for designing the book so well, in spite of my preference for dodgy, unfocused images; Billy Childish; L-13; BAR; Steve Lowe; David Jenkins; Robert Grose; the many lexicographers and authors whose dictionaries I have consulted; my art history tutor at Hornsey College of Art, John A. Walker; Dr Albirt Umber; Harold Rosenbloom; J. J. Charlesworth; AICA-UK; Michael Curran and Tangerine Press for the specialist binding on the limited edition; Susan Corke for her assistance with the drypoint edition made for the same; Great Western Studios for providing me a studio-office; Al Lobb at 38 Squadron; and Victoria Grant and Theodora Brown for being loving and kind.

Finally, I would like to state the continuance of my own true belief in **artists**. I thank them all, especially the many fantastic and fabulous ones who have chosen to work with me over the years.

A

abecedarium A popular glass fronted, temperature controlled vitrine receptacle for the language of art. See → **dictionary**

abjection See → **autocannibalism**

abstinence, art Usually theoretical model only of a locus avoidment strategy, sometimes part of a holiness principle, usually attempted by staying at home while others practice exuberant self harm rituals, at art openings or the art party. Authorities agree that probably more avoidance holiness is gained from the avoidance of the art fair than the art party. Holiness has also been claimed for avoiding other entertainments, such as viewing the Olympic Games opening ceremony on television. See also → **silence**, **stillness**, **hope**.

absolute, the See → **Hegel**

absurd counterpoint A singularity addition placed in conjunction within or about a larger work – usually an installation or sculpture – by which the work is given a literal or symbolic difference of subject-object (or scale) values. See → **theatricality in art**

abyss A very low substratum, beneath which are devils.

academic The principal locus variant of an unremitting variant locus.

accidental idea A super locus effect occurs when someone stares obsessively at a part of an idea and then looks away. He or she will temporarily perceive a part of the new locus idea in a similar shape as the first, but as a complementary one: ie if the original idea was negative or cynical or melancholy, the apparent shape is positive or optimistic or joyful. See → **seeing**

aesthetic judgement Jocular term. See → **beautiful**, **lovely**, **wonderful**.

afterbirth Status VIP dining foodstuff.

addict, classical cannabinoids model A locus value that is congruent with a particularising discourse often considered a psychopharmacological grammar, based on the classical cannabinoids. Such a grammar is usually a metapsychology derived from the pluralisms determined by what some authorities have called **dimensions of intersubjectivity**. In the twentieth century certain thinker-authors shared an experimental usage of the drug Cannabis sativa, with consequent mental experiences of discontinuous vacillation of meaning, revealed (in the late morning) as a theoretical locus value in their writings, about which they were very excited, as they understood non-cognitive psychosisism to be an addition to meaning. Artists have been influenced in a secondary or tertiary codependency of these values, based on their understandings of these writings, through which is created important and esteemed art, highly favoured by arts professionals. See → **religious impulse**, **occupational psychosis**.

advertising An important and much loved locus value that replaces abandonment.

aesthetics The philosophy of art with regard to locus criteria either with or without rules.

altarpiece Contemporary art has repeatedly offered presentational constructs summoning locus displacement ideas of reverence and homage, often appropriating variant religious object vocabularies, such as the altarpiece and the shrine. Often exhibited in dim light or near darkness. See → **religious impulse**

amateur conceptual art An ironic, relaxing, popular art hobby greatly enjoyed by millions of ironic people, of all social classes and ironic ability levels. The contemporary version of Victorian watercolour painting or Sunday painting.

ambiguity Common locus trope.

ambition See → **aura**

amulet Occasional locus trope.

anaphora A device of visual rhetoric, in which repetitions, sometimes incremental, create a cumulative effect for little apparent effort (or, jocularly, create a vast disproportionality of effort for little cumulative effect). See → **cliché**, **stereotype**.

animal in art See → **canapé**, **hybridism**.

anoint Common locus trope.

anticlimax A common effect device in which is made dramatic a (usually) digressive banality, whose technique has become a classic stereotype not unrelated to a form of militant apathy of purpose. Residing within this, in what sometimes seems to be an infinity of regressive processes, is the deliberated expiry locus of the shaggy dog story. See → **absurd counterpoint**, **futility**, **infantilism**, **cliché**, **stereotype**.

antipath An antipath is someone whose dislike of contemporary art amounts to an actual terror, and which is expressed in distressed, unintelligible exclamations while leaping upwards at hard surfaces from the dinner table.

anus Here is meant the 'active' mirroring anus of ineffable high jouissance, rather than the 'passive' anus – the active anus not just the beingness centre of unconstrained delimitation, but also an ejaculating matrix – a vehicle for displacement interventions of metabolic and generative (the fecal embryo) illimitability

anxiety See → **abjection**

apathy A euphemistic behaviour term, used by or about young artists, that signifies an extreme ambition syndrome.

apocalypse Common locus trope.

arabesque Curvature locus.

archaism The appropriation of earlier art and design styles is often an ironic retro-usage, or fascination homage, but is more usually a stylistic ostentation stratagem masquerading as a false value locus. See → **irony**, **cliché**, **stereotype**.

art An often theoretically lurid novelty transfer-object, constructed or 'found' so as to command a confusedly fascinated orienting response. Orientation is the initial usage value; bio-socially, art is similar to a dog's bark, or a pig's grunt. Authorities are agreed that these are the universal definition values shared by everything that is known as art. It has been observed, however, that it is as slaughtered flesh that a farm animal becomes valuable. See → **art fair**, **death**.

artist See → **artworld**

art fair A system of replicating wooden booths densely situated within an artificially lit, barnlike construction. Within the demarcated territory values of each booth is a dealer, often physically very large and florid, or sometimes very thin with a sniffly nose. The booths are situated on parallel lines that appear to meet at the furthest point of a perspectival infinity. At this imaginary point status foodstuffs are made available, later violently excreted out of the windows of courtesy cars onto the roads, where cheeky sparrows may pick through the ordure matter for new ideas. See → **trickle down effect**

art magazine A coded validation document by means of which hierarchies of meaning (See → **artworld**) may either be furthered or restricted. See → **advertising rates**

artworld A capitalistic value order system in which the transfer objects known as art are exchanged, so enabling those engaged in the exchange – principally bankers (See → **collector**) and dealers, served by artists – to acquire forms of social merit. If bankers succeed in gaining sufficient merit from dealers, they may then be permitted to deposit their sperm inside the artists, either vaginally or within the walls of the rectum.

ascension See → **addict, cannabis model.**

ashes A specific and highly valued form of dust. See → **particulates**

ass The locus buttocks area of the critic, in the deep centre of which is the tightly closed anus. Ass may also refer to the animal known as the donkey, in the centre of which there is also an anus, but which is a nicer one. The critic may be the emblem of darkness and devilish inclination, and is a known obstacle between the spiritually disenchanted and the godhead.

attitude It is always a good idea to show curiosity, playfulness, affection, sociality and to have an innate desire to cooperate.

aura See → **solar being**

authority It is axiomatic that only the art critic has the right to do or demand something in respect of art, including the absolute right to demand that other people do what he or she says. This is by virtue of the critic's rational-legal, traditional and charismatic authority.

auto-cannibalism See → **anxiety**

avant-garde A taboo term, based on discovered skull fragment origins now previously lost, soon to be found again.

avarice A psychological momentum characteristic of art practice that is related to sucking.

axis The distance between the exact centre of the art gallery and the exact centre of heaven. See → **sky**

B

baa-ing Lazy, locus term for universal response to 'blockbuster' shows. See → **meat byproducts**

baboon A large monkey with a long face, doglike teeth, large lip and buttock callosities. Vocal in expressing its dislike of good **contemporary art**. Baboons may write negatively about art for **newspapers** or **broadcast media**. When on TV, can be seen putting its fingers in its own ano-genital region and then carefully bringing them to the **nose** to smell. Will charge a small fee for public appearances, with which it buys **drink**. When on **radio**, will display dislike by deep grunting and noisily expectorating.

bad art The enjoyment of poor quality, bad art is a form of high-locus context exhilaration in the presence of incompetence and failure, in many instances related to liminal performativity. It is fundamentally enjoyed unconditionally within the simple locus of the 'fail' category, but may be theorised upwards. Approving reference to bad art is a commonplace, and should lead to mimetic crisis – and, for over eighty years, it has. See → **camp**

banana Herbaceous perennial plant. Standard locus trope signifier used particularly in 1990s contemporary art practice. Locus substitute signifier for the infant Christ's **penis**. See → **Steinberg** (*The Sexuality of Christ in Renaissance Art and in Modern Oblivion*).

banishment A locus consequence of transgressive breaches of coded artworld dominance locus hierarchy systems, in which the banished are a) denied art press attention, b) denied important eye contact at art openings and c) denied access to secret cocaine (benzoylmethylecgonine) rituals, all thus leading to professional **death**.

banquet See → **dance of death**, **vomit (return to)**.

baroque The Baroque was a characteristic locus artistic style of the seventeenth century; the term is also a recontextualised ahistorical paradigm summary pejorative imprecation locus that seeks to describe ordinate complication made for its own sake. Used in respect of false kinds of high intellectual ecstasy, in which it is claimed the artist overwhelms his or her audience with an appeal to knowledge formulas complicated by ornamental rhetoric theologies. (See also → **hidden key**) Such art is vilified. However, it should be noted that all authorities agree that both the artist-agent antagonists and bellicose-victim-complainant audiences of such art are parties to a mutually pleasurable bargain, in which each may claim a high piety locus status payoff, and in which both are co-equally complicit. Other colluding parties in what is a triangulating pact situation are the curatorial and arts administration authorities who encourage antagonist-victim (and **baboon**) strategies so as to further their own piety agendas in respect of audience and **funding** categories, based on expanded social energy targets.

barylalia Indistinct 'thick' speech and/or poor articulation. See → **pub** (US bar) and **baboon**.

basketry A basket is a woven container made of materials such as wood, reed, cane, rattan or rush, often with a handle or handles. It is usually light in weight. Among the commonly used basketry techniques are plaiting, twining and coiling. Parts of a basket include the base, the side walls and rim. A basket may have a lid and handle. Basketry is one of the oldest of crafts. The gendered basket is the artist's **handbag**. The basket may be a symbol of the **womb** or locus **anus**.

bastard Art critical term for locus excitement values.

bath See → **urinal**

beauty Once an approbation term now made critically absent through a broad consensus of distaste so as to be almost (and sometimes literally) a locus prohibition. Occasionally reappears with great novelty and neo-effect value. Paradoxically, without a viable socialised usage of the term 'beautiful', there cannot be an avant-garde, and certainly not a beautiful one.

bed The most common installation prop. Usually metal, usually shown in low light, without mattress. Aural accompaniment will always have **reverb**.

belief It is claimed in various belief propositions that all artists share a belief in faith.

benefactor A benefactor is one whose greatest desire is not to be discovered using his or her wealth in a quiet assisting of **joy**, **purpose** and **meaning** in the world.

bestiality A common theme among both male and female video artists, but with a slight bias drift towards the female.

bewilderment Many art-critical terms are locus embarrassment synonyms for bewilderment, which is a term commonly avoided, as it implies a diminished knowledge status. See → **sublime**

biennial (biennale) A replicating number of identical art events, so common as needing to be kept geographically and durationally ringfenced. Attended by a number of replicating people, saying replicating things. Important persons may physically appear at more than one biennial at exactly the same time.

bird Symbol of opposition to the **serpent**, representing **heaven**. Some female birds may shit on their male partner's car **windscreen**.

bite See → **critical response**

bisexual A bisexual usually takes place every two years. Politicians and civic functionaries support them as they assist in the regeneration of urban areas.

blind contour drawing See → **body**

black An absolute **colour**. See → **Uncle Tom's Cabin**, **Auschwitz hut**.

blaming See → **blessing**

blessing It is a blessing to make good art, or to help make good art, or to see good art. In this way a person may approach holiness, the highest form of cosmic energy.

blot Projective test devised by Rorschach based on his viewing the shape his wet testicles made when he stood up from sitting on a seat after bathing. Many artists have explored testicular forms in their practice.

blue A lovely, lovely colour, good for children to look at.

body A site of meaning, commencing at the anus and terminating everywhere else.

bones Without question, the most common art installation prop and locus signifier. Some artists think the soul is contained within the bones, or that they may come to life again. See → **skull worship**

book locus term for a **text**.

boredom The most common durational strategy locus in video art. Given emphasis by virtue of either no seats being provided, or hard, uncomfortable ones with no backs.

bowels Intestines. Known to have magical powers, and usually preserved in an **art storage** facility after death. It has been said that demons and monsters may try to steal the jar, but this has been proved untrue, as they are usually **burned** instead.

bricolage A locus process by which, in the same way a pig becomes pork when served for dinner, so bric-a-brac becomes bricolage when it has a catalogue essay and footnotes written about it.

breast See → **female supremacy**, **Klein**.

bread See → **ritual**

brown A lovely, lovely colour representative of infinite contemplative wisdom and humility. Also the colour of the locus **cigar** sometimes used by painters to represent extreme **Freudian sadism** in the context of violent **anal rape**.

brushwork The most common art material of all is white paint, of which it is estimated that over 100 billion gallons are used yearly worldwide, to paint gallery walls. No brushstrokes are apparent, as paint is applied using rollers.

bubbles a) An extremely thin film of soapy water enclosing exciting ideas that form a sphere with an iridescent surface. Often used for children's enjoyment, but also in artistic performances b) a painting by J. E. Millais, used to advertise the **Conservative and Unionist Party**, which caused controversy about the relationship between art, advertising, and bubbles. The controversy is still continuing, with bubbles usually deemed to be winning.

bullfighting See → **Robert Hughes**, **gnat**.

bureaucracy Many artists instigate self-generated bureaucracies in which they fetishise unnecessary organising statements and conceptual models. This is similar to the process in which, it is said, victims can themselves become abusers.

butterfly See → **bullfighting**, **gnat**.

buttocks See → **anus**

C

camp See → **connoisseurship**

cannibalism The most prevalent of the cannibalisms in contemporary art is the **autoconsumption** by artists of their own blood, penis, faeces or other bodily materiality. The literal killing and eating of others is less common, although the blood, faeces or other bodily materiality of an artist may be offered to others to share. The radical transformations of the strategies of documentation are thus engaged in the reconstruction of a continuum: an operation in narrative time which is physically affected by memory and history, and where past and future are reconstituted as present. See also → **vomit (return to)**

car design in art It is a truism that modern car design is now based on the caricature vehicles used by the bad guys in comic books, which are conspicuously oppressive and threatening when driven around art galleries, by virtue of their improbable size and bullying musculature. Such cars are usually **black**.

catalogue Publication with essay, illustrations, etc, published by a public or private **gallery**, the text written by a **hysteric**. Because catalogues are an advertisement, they have a compromised critical independence. Where the artist is alive, they are deemed to have no critical independence whatsoever. See → **advertising**, **bubbles**.

celebrity See → **buttocks**

chain Common locus art trope.

children's (youth) art Both Charles Dickens and Paul and Iona **Opie** wrote descriptively about cheeky young, nineteenth century 'East End Cockney' artists, many little more than children, and how they could be seen dancing, selling art, eating winkles and sniffing **cocaine** (benzoylmethylecgonine) powder from colourful baskets (See also → **basketry**) as they cried their wares in London streets. See → **Lionel Bart**, **Fagin**, **Poor Law Amendment Act of 1834**.

chimpanzee See also → **baboon**. Humans share 98 percent of their DNA with the chimpanzee, but **dealers** will only share 50 percent plus framing costs.

chora See → **ciborium**

ciborium Liturgical vessel used to hold the Eucharist.

cinema a) A cultural locus accorded reverence by theorists, in which the radical transformations of the strategies of documentation are engaged in the reconstruction of a continuum: an operation in narrative time which is physically affected by memory and history, and where past and future are reconstituted as present. b) A socialised locus of architectural space showing a film of very long duration, in which actors mime sex, and where the audiences sit in foul dirt and darkness, consuming fatty foodstuffs, expelling silent **fartage**.

city See → **Babylon**

classicism Certain formulas have been devised so as to attempt definition of this term whose normative value usage is a variable depending on historical and descriptive context. The radical transformations of the strategies of documentation are thus engaged in the reconstruction of a continuum: an operation in narrative time which is physically affected by memory and history, and where past and future are reconstituted as present.

cliché Clichés tend to be 'classical' clichés, and are therefore important vocabulary modes. Without clichés there is no comprehension, and arts professionals would have no common language or ability to function. The radical transformations of the strategies of documentation are thus engaged in the reconstruction of a continuum: an operation in narrative time which is physically affected by memory and history, and where past and future are reconstituted as present.

cluster fuck US military slang term for intractable disarray (often involving multiple deaths) now appropriated by practitioners of the **hey dude** style of art writing. There is a corresponding tendency for the military to borrow art-critical, hey-dude terms in return, such as '**visual discourse**' – used, for example, to describe the **aerial bombing** of **peasant villages**.

clown Extremely common locus trope in contemporary art especially in its relationship to the dominant jocular **banana locus**.

cock Universal symbol for the rising solar penis.

cocaine (benzoylmethylecgonine) A crystalline tropane alkaloid. An art material unusually characterised by a transversality of specialisation. See → **toilet**, **urinal**.

coda See → **absurd counterpoint**

code See → **hidden key**

colour A universal positive in visual art. With the exception, some authorities claim, of much 1970s practice. Colours are present in nature freely, but may be withdrawn from art, only being returned for a fee. See → **red**, **yellow**, **green**, **blue**, **indigo**, **violet**.

column See → **Godhead**

compassion See → **heart**

conceptual art The relationship of the determined commodity object, or thought locus, within the statement terms of a directive authorial strategy.

confessional art See → **drunk, mum, dad.**

connoisseurship See → **big black cock, anus.**

contrariety See → **culture**

craquelure See → **anus, connoisseurship.**

critic See → **critical theory**

critical theory The commonly accepted theory that art critics must be in compliance with, and write favourably about, an artist or exhibition on the basis of the written commands of an **important press release**.

critique See → **hidden key**

culture See → **contrariety**

cunt See → **chora**

cuts A jocular locus term, usually part of a fiscal transformation strategy implemented by politicians. Cuts may be used for the torture and execution of living artists or arts organisations, or applied as an act of humiliation after death. Cuts are generally to the arms, legs, and chest leading to **amputation** of limbs, followed by **decapitation** or a stab to the **heart**. If the executioner is merciful, the first cut is to the throat causing death, subsequent cuts serving solely to dismember the corpse. Politicians may celebrate cuts as being the juxtaposition of divine ecstasy and extreme horror, thus leading to a lifelong search for a form of the **sacred** that is beyond the understanding of the civilised world.

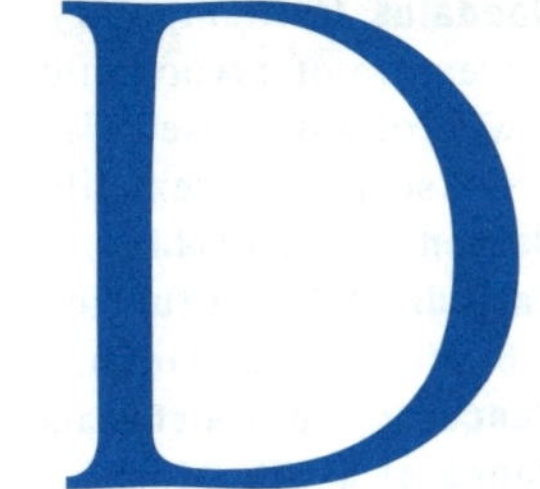

Daedalus Contemporary Greek artist. Known for his skillful creation of a wooden cow in which his patron, Pasiphaë (the wife of a deceased Greek shipping magnate), concealed herself so as to be sexually penetrated by a **bull**.

Deinon See → **daffodil**

daffodil A beautiful flower with a primal yellow form. Painted by Vincent van Gogh, who also painted irises and sunflowers.

dance See → **dance of death**

dance of death Most high social functions, held in both state and private art institutions, may be described using this term. See → **convulsion**, **prance**.

darkness The absence of light has metaphorical significance in many cultures, and is therefore the means to create a signature discourse in respect of either the meta-relations of a stasis unity, or an unbecoming locus-praxis disunity. The showing of artists' videos in near darkness is a summary process of this index of re-presence; a locusment of technology redundancy which exists, with teleological significance, for exaggerated theatrical effect only. Thus it is often considered a strident presentational **affectation** of locus causality with the likelihood of some handbag theft occurring.

Dasein See → **Deinon**

Davy's grey A greenish-grey pigment, made from powdered slate, iron oxide and carbon black. Granular and transparent, it is sometimes difficult to handle because of its tendency to **clump**.

dealer A buyer and seller of art. Dealers may use a loud sing-song cry or chant to attract attention. The dealer in London is subject to regulation by law, under the administration of the Commissioner of the Metropolitan Police. If the dealer's gallery is stationary, by-laws of local councils also apply. Legislation exists under clause six of the Metropolitan Streets Act 1867, which deals with obstruction by goods to pavements (sidewalks) and streets. There are various modern amendments. See → **whelks**

death Although artists often kill themselves, each other or other people, it remains unusual for them to be actually killed for making bad art. The conclusion usually drawn from this, that art is not actually that important, tends to be an insulting one to artists. Historically artists have salvaged dignity by giving emphasis to strategies that may lead them to being ignored, and thus perishing in great pain through loss of livelihood. See also → **cuts**

deconstruction See → **pun**

delirium See → **dementia**

dementia See → **delirium**

demons Evil spirits, or the servants of Satan.

demonstrative rhetoric code Signaling imploration behaviours based on **scent** that successfully draw attention to an artist being erudite, learned and so cognisant with theory tendencies as to be given reciprocating critical approval validation responses in return.

deposition The taking down of Jesus Christ from the **cross**.

derision Term used in respect of certain cultural imprecation contexts, in which derisive insults are an important value norm.

détournement See → **dance of death**

deviance Deviancies in contemporary art now tend to be omissive.

Diana Blink The movements of the eyelids made famous by **Princess Diana**. A visible form of defiant status valiance, now a cultural epitome locus and given a leveraged meaning sentiment equivalence in certain kinds of contemporary art practice, often with emphasis on a mascara equivalent summoning process. Such a discourse elevates and attenuates otherwise excluded or marginalised notions of moral justice, and consequent resentments in an assertioning of disbarred categories of sentiment meaning.

diary A very common art installation trope, referencing approved validation formulas.

diorama A common art installation trope, referencing approved validation formulas.

disbelief See → **cuts**

disco A common art installation trope, referencing approved validation formulas.

dissociation An abnormal mental state in which the subject's perception of phenomena may differ remarkably from that of others. See → **film critic**

diversity See → **love**

documentary A common art installation trope, referencing approved validation formulas.

dominance Aggressive behaviour, often ritualised. Usually ceases when the threatened individual is seen to submit and agree that the art previously stated as disliked is in fact excellent (or even wonderful). Domination occurs through clothing ostentation, status meals, phallic symbolism etc.

donor A patron or benefactor of gifts and bequests. By these means donors gain delivery from the **pox**, enjoy victory in war and achieve release from captivity in military defeat, etc. They also get to **give it up the arse** to young artists.

drawing Unusual art strategy device in which stylus materials are appropriated so as to make marked lines on flat paper in a correspondence with a visually perceived external reality.

Duchamp American artist. **Transvestite**. Known for the conflicted hypersexuality of his art practice. His emphasis on hairless **genital partialism** and isolationist autoeroticism has made him popular with audiences all over the world. Played chess, a game with an intense psychological quality of deception and introspectiveness which in some respects is analogous to the intimate identity displacings of autoerotic transvestism. Duchamp also employed the recursive **pun**, by which he compounded the locus genderments and regenderments of dissociative sociosexuality. Paradoxically, although Duchamp has many followers, very few of them are transvestite or play chess, and consequently they lack proper understanding of his work. Academic followers are invariably sexually inactive, and thus lack any understanding whatsoever. See → **erotica**, **parnomasia**.

dumbing down See → **dumbing up**

dysfunctional The opposite of functional. Dysfunctional is generally regarded as better and more interesting.

Dystopia Imaginary country (jocular) with a proud arts tradition.

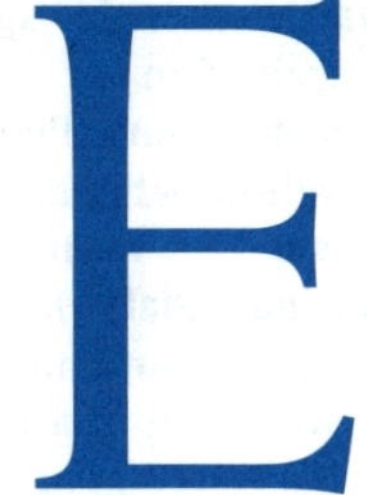

ear Authorities agree that a portrait in profile is always a portrait of an ear.

earth colours Pigments that are obtained by mining, such as yellow ochre and umber.

easel See → **vomit (return to)**

eating ritual The eating of the body of a god is known as theophagy, and may be performed symbolically through the consumption of a food or symbolic material. In fertility rituals, harvested grain may be the reborn god of vegetation, known as **canapés**. Paradoxically, canapés actually inhibit fertility as they may make the breath smell repugnant, or small pieces of them may fall within the groin of the trousers (if male), or onto the bosom (if female).

echinus An architectural term describing the convex element of a capital that is directly below the abacus.

eclecticism A systemic style system with a feigned variousness indicator strategy locus variant.

edit culture It is common in literary publishing for a work to be so changed by editorial process and publicity that the author becomes a coequal with, or even secondary to, the editor and publisher. In contemporary art, a dealer (moving slowly, so as to have an almost undetectable pulse), may determine the form and presentation of artwork, in such a way as to confer aura context valuement status to an artist. Thus the gallery/curator may become the brandment locus rather than the art or artist.

efflorescence An excited variegated coloured blotching on the faces of the rich at the moment of purchase of an artwork costing over 10 million (dollars, pounds or euros).

emperor's new clothes See → **schlock**, **schmutter**.

emerald green A common name for copper acetoarsenite, or CI pigment green 21, an extremely toxic blue-green chemical, used by **Monet**, **Van Gogh** and **Cézanne**. Ingestion causes vesicle formation and eventual sloughing of the mucosa in the mouth, pharynx and oesophagus. Also abdominal pain, cyanosis, bloody **diarrhoea**, weakness, spasms, hypothermia, **delirium**, **coma**, convulsions, acute tubular **necrosis** and **death**.

emporiatrics The branch of medicine that deals with those health problems that may affect international travellers. Also a common locus art-tendency characterised by appropriations of airport architecture and travel signage (and enervated qualities of desensitised fatigue), which may come to constitute a subject locus for a highly important, influential, well respected **curator**. See → **flight**

entasis An almost imperceptible convex tapering (an apparent swelling) in the shaft of a column. See also → **yoni**

epigraphy The study of written inscriptions. In contemporary art exhibitions, the display captions accompanying exhibits are often revered for their textual mastery.

epic A commonplace device in contemporary art whereby more (bigger, larger, taller, etc) is considered to be a value in its own right, simply by virtue of locus scale increasement. See also → **awesome**

equality locus paradox An essential contestability paradigm empathy posit. For example, if well-intentioned arts professional A were to postulate that 'all persons are equally intelligent', and if the response from well intentioned arts professional B were 'I am too stupid to understand the postulate' then that would be both not stupid, and too stupid, at the same time.

ethnicity Green trolls who write letters to liberal newspapers on the subject of ethnicity in the arts invariably describe their own skin colouring as being either white or black.

ethyl alcohol. See → **kebab, vomit (return to).**

evaluation The arts are evaluated by artists, critics, collectors, curators, dealers, administrators, bureaucrats, etc, but not by the taxpaying public. In 2005 it was proposed that a National Visual Arts Audiences Association be formed, so as to represent the public interest in respect of art and culture as presented by publicly funded arts bodies such as galleries and museums. It was imagined that the NVAAA would comment on exhibition standards, admission charges, catering and exhibition catalogues (including spot checks for intelligibility). Public arts bodies responded with alarmed hostility to this proposal, claiming that their own board of council members should be counted as members of the public instead. The scheme went into abeyance after an NVAAA committee member was kidnapped, tortured and murdered by the director of a major public gallery.

evil eye See → **critic**

excess See → **efflorescence**

excrement See → **excellence**

executive desktop toy art A category of art predicated on novelty values of the plaything entertainments that executives place on their desks. Desktop art is scaled up to be physically huge and costly, but is completely identical in principle to its original model, except less fun.

exhibition, special A special art exhibition is a show of art in a public gallery's dark, remote, basement area, in distinction to its gift shop, which enjoys prestigious, just-off-centre placement on the ground floor.

experimental See → **vomit (return to)**

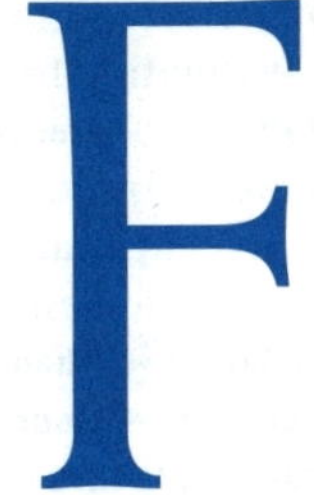

fable A common art installation trope, referencing approved validation formulas.

face See → **prosopagnosia**

faeces Intense, slow-drying paste material of high (See → **fine art**) cultural specificity with a recurrent approval-usage locus endorsement in art practice.

failure See → **happiness**, **schadenfreude**.

fake See → **sincerity**

fancy picture A term applied in the eighteenth century to sentimental, usually rural, genre scene pictures. Peasants may be idealised, and there is a sense of artificial contrivance about such works. Now replaced by **porn**.

farce See → **art prize**, **baboon**.

fashion See → **skull**, **rib cage**, **jawbone**.

fat Occasional art locus trope.

feelings The secret touchings of the **sexy area** of the loved one at the boring **vernissage**.

fellatio Oral sex act performed upon a **male**. When performed upon a **female**, oral sex is called cunnilingus. Oral sex is claimed by certain theorists to be a measurable unit of socio-evolutionary obligation, and of special interest in relation to determinant values in cultural practice. Opinions differ as to how best to apply the concept of oral sex within a proper disciplinary framework, although there is now an increasingly precise understanding of what is involved. Proponents argue that a consideration of cultural developments *as if* oral sex itself had an eye view (as if oral sex itself responded to pressure to maximise its own replication and survival), can lead to useful insights and yield valuable predictions into how culture (and cultural patronage) develops over time. See also → **muff dive**

feminism See → **female supremacy**, **muff dive**.

feminist criticism See → **female supremacy**

feminist theology See → **female supremacy**

fetishism See → **ficelle**

ficelle Term used by Henry James to describe a minor lesbian sexual fetishist and/or a minor male **coprophiliac** in a catalogue essay, whose conversations with the protagonist serve to provide background information for the reader. See → **cultural theorist**, **art critic**, **art historian**.

fine art See → **free-market capitalism**

fire Locus traditional carpet **burn** on an artist's knees or buttocks may be caused by either sexual friction, or psychotropic **convulsion**, or both. See → **hellfire**

fish Fish are symbolic of fish.

fixation See → **Freud**, **psychoanalysis**.

flame See → **fire**

flâneur A common art critical locus trope, referencing approved validation formulas. See → ***City of Dreadful Night***

flashback See → ***Civilisation*** **(TV series)**

flight A common art trope that references a multiplicity simultaneity locus of both arrival *and* departure referencing curatorially approved system validation formulas relating to libidinous power in the sky. See → **god**, **neurotic**, **dream**, **aspiration**.

flesh A common art locus trope, referencing approved validation formulas.

flood Symbolic signifier of spiritual leakiness.

flower Beautiful natural plant form. See → **Burra, Edward**

folk art, folklore The collective wisdom of the 'folk' – customs, beliefs, pithy stories, rituals, games, dances, songs, legends, myths, tales, proverbs, sayings, violently anti-semitic or homophobic football chants, etc.

folly Architectural term. A synonym for site-specific, **installation** (or sometimes **intervention**) art.

fool See → **folly**

forensic medicine A common art trope, referencing approved validation formulas.

formalism A pejorative term in Soviet art criticism. See → **alcoholism**

formulaic system Commonplace conformity to stock arts-professional idea locus narratives, especially those that reference approved locus validation criteria of locus specificity.

found object A common art trope, referencing approved validation formulas.

fragment A common art trope, referencing approved validation formulas.

free association See → **Freud**, **fixation**, **fellatio**.

free-market capitalism See → **faeces**

Freud, Sigmund Author of a book about Leonardo da Vinci.

Freud sought, unsuccessfully, to assert his supremacy over Leonardo, the incomparably greater genius, by subjecting him to a retrospective analysis which included disparagements related to oral sex (See → **fellatio**). Freud's book is regarded as an unintentionally humorous one because of being based on a gross mistranslation of a Leonardo text. After his discovery of the mistranslation, Freud said regretfully of his book that 'it is the only beautiful thing I have ever written'.

friend-substitution strategy A pragmatic analysis technique by which boring art is made more interesting to the viewer by imagining it has been created by a close personal friend, especially someone the viewer wishes to have **sexual intercourse** with.

fuscous A dark, drab colour. May refer to the olive, leaden or similar dark colouring of the coarse woven clothes traditionally worn by both art historians and art critics. If scholar-academics then these tend to be heavily bearded, especially the females, and either violently Marxist or violently Conservative. Dried egg yolk is often found on the clothing of both, presenting as a yellowish ingress within the rough fibres that clothe the upper chest (thorax) area or, as a variant, resting upon the surface fabric fibres in a glistening, golden impasto. Both males and females may smell of fishy paté foodstuffs, usually purchased from **Waitrose**. See → **fustian**

fustian See → **fuscous**

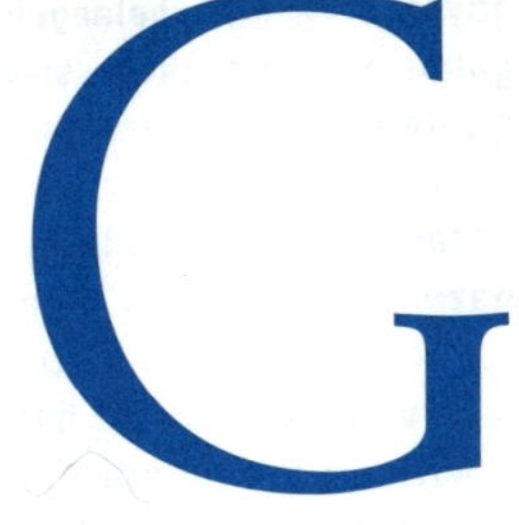

gay art See → **Michelangelo of Finland**

game See → **art**, **chess**, **struggle**, **death**.

garden Earthly paradise ... cosmos ... spiritual correspondence ... See → **expulsion**...

gateway Common locus trope. See → **Duchamp**

gaze The gaze may be placed in relation to the **evil eye**. Charms and decorations featuring the eye are a common sight in gallery gift shops and have become a popular choice of souvenir with art-loving murderers and rapists. Thus, the gaze either is, or is not, part of culture. In this way is opened up a discussion about the privileges of transcendental space, and the displacement of the so-called dimension of inter-subjectivity, and its relationship with the pre-objective, primordial world.

gender See → **gonads**

genetic assimilation (art) Arises when: a) dominant **baboon** members of a civic population dislike contemporary art, and bay and strut indignantly before it; b) this population's response is selected naturally (or artificially) as part of a wider biosocial process; c) the accumulation of predisposing factors comes to favour an inheritance of the response. Such populations will then bay and strut (or prance) in an indignant neurology, even in the absence of any art environmental stimulus.

genre A conservative trope locus categorisation system with a recognised level of generalised organisation pattern characteristics, sometimes with locus variant subgenres that appear diverse, but which may overall constitute a strict rule set. For example, the human skeleton is the privileged species-centric nominate of a taxonomically locused necro-genre, within which reside sublocus variants that include the dog, bat, mouse, pig and bird skeletons. See → **taxonomy**, **skull**.

geometry In terms of pictorial composition, the placement or arrangement of visual elements. In religious art, composition tends to be symmetrical. As symmetry is so conducive to meditative purposefulness, many authorities claim that all symmetrical art (including sculpture) is religious art. See → **minimalism**

ghost artist Someone, usually a dealer or curator, who anonymously arranges the creation of an artist's work, sometimes in accordance with the artist's wishes, so advancing the artist's **genius**.

Gill, Eric (1842–1940) English engraver, letter-cutter, sculptor, typographer and writer. Carvings and other works of his are in the Tate. Will be best remembered for **fucking** his sisters, daughters and a **dog**.

Giotto (1266–1337) A Florentine painter whose works are imbued with high poetic beauty.

glory In Christian art, a term that describes the radiance that surrounds a sacred figure.

glory hole In sexual slang a glory hole describes a hole in a wall between cubicles in a public toilet. Through this hole an engorged dealer will insert his or her artist for contact with a collector. See → **mandorla**

glossolalia Speaking in tongues. The vocalising or the writing of speechlike syllables about art sometimes occurs, often as part of a meta-religious practice. Though many consider these utterances to be meaningless, others believe them to be a holy language, as indeed they are.

God The Great Geometrician of the Universe. See → **minimalism**, **symmetry**.

Gogh, Vincent van Important painter and writer of high religious sensibility. Alcoholic self-harmer.

gold Reflective metal. In many places, gold is believed to be highly important, but it is not.

golden calf. Prime infant suckling cow, roasted alive in real gold, and served with a dish of young broad beans. The epidermal layer of each individual bean is removed by swearing Asian kitchen workers (See → **minimum wage**), who then drizzle warmed fresh spunk oil (both gay and straight) upon the tender surfaces.

golden section (golden mean) A proportion (8:13) regarded as having harmonic aesthetic virtue, and which can be found in most works of art. Sometimes said to be **irrational**.

gonads in art The development of gonads is a part of the development of the urinary and reproductive organs. The gonad is the organ that makes gametes. The gonads in male artists are the testicles, and the gonads in female artists are the ovaries. The product, gametes, are haploid germ cells. For example, spermatozoon and egg cells are gametes.

gothic See → **green**

gothic international Stylistic offshoot of gothic.

graphic art Most contemporary fine art comprises expository diagrams and is therefore, according to the most authorities, **graphic art**.

great chains of being Classificatory systems that map experience are common to all worldviews and scientific theories. In the artworld, classifications tend to relate to a hierarchy that includes the **invitation**, the private view, the post-private-view dinner, and the post-private-view-after-dinner drinks party. Authorities agree that to arrive at a post-private-view-after-dinner-drinks party without having been invited to the post-private-view dinner (usually not having realised that such a dinner was taking place) is to be publicly exposed as being a lower **monkey** in the **Great Chain of Being** than if one had only gone to the private view.

green A nice **colour**. There are more discernible multiplicity variations of green than any other hue.

grey A nice **colour**. When a painter needs to put paint on an area of canvas, but does not know which colour, and if a critic is not available to advise them, then it is usually best to use grey.

grotesque A term that is not, in its technical sense, related to normal usage. Abnormal usage is to be preferred.

guild An association for the regulation and training of artists. After a period of apprenticeship and general practice, an artist might apply to become a master. See → **Groucho Club**, **Colony**, **death**.

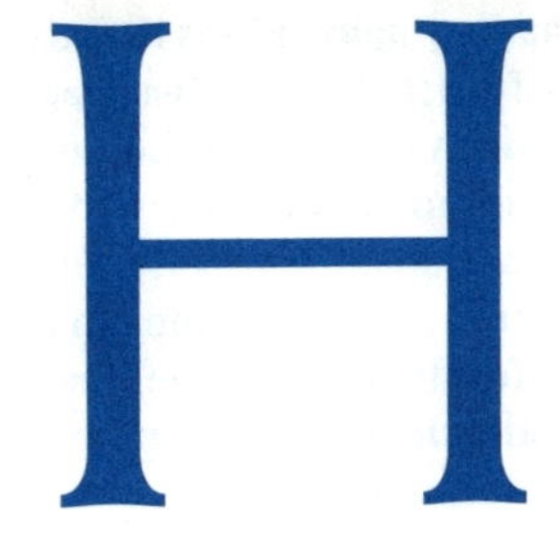

hagiography Pious literature about a hugely important, wonderful artist. See → **monograph**

hair A once overly common locus-specific art trope referencing approved validation formulas, but now fallen into relative disuse, apart from reference to pubic hair, a contemporary locus trope that functions in a similar way that long female hair did for the Pre-Raphaelites.

hallucination A common art trope, referencing approved validation formulas.

happening Preferred term for an old-fashioned multimedia installation event.

harlot A female sex worker. Mayhew describes the common London sight of a crying and trouserless critic whose traditionally small quantity of cocaine powder has been taken from them by a prostitute (traditionally female, but sometimes male, occasionally a bit of both), whose accomplices have then beaten the critic up for the traditional pleasure of it.

Harry See → **Pye, Harry**

hat Many persons in the art world wear hats, especially those suffering from alcohol abuse problems. For these persons a hat indicates a reaching for spiritual meaning.

hate An exquisite, self-validating form of emotion or feeling that displaces troubling anxiety and doubt. Often actuates the social conditions in which art is perceived. See → **love**

hate speech Unacceptable usage terms about art such as **interesting**, nice, attractive, etc.

head Depictions of ritualistic decapitation (sometimes including public display of the severed head) have been common throughout art history. Severance of the head may be fatal to artists, as brain death can occur within minutes without circulating oxygenated blood.

heart An extremely common art trope, now usually used in locus respect of a reference to traditional tattoo signage.

heaven A common art trope, referencing approved validation formulas. See → **PR consultancy**

hegemony See → **organic intellectuals of the ruling class**

hell See → **hospitality**

hermeneutics Theory of interpretation and analysis, which may include reference to locus context ideals of excretion value meanings. Contemporary opinion denies a determinate reading of such a meaning.

hip See → **hop**

hippy A common art trope, referencing approved validation formulas.

Hobsbawm, Eric Distinguished historian. Wrote using a curious, disagreeable syntax.

hog Porcine. See → **dealer**

homoerotic See → **St Francis Bacon of Finland**

hop See → **hopeless**

hope See → **truth**, **justice**, **beauty**.

horror A common art trope, now generally used in respect of cartoon bones, skulls etc.

hospitality According to most theorists the VIP lounge is the disguised entrance to hell, which is Satan's kingdom, and where torment is by **demons**.

Household Responsibility System Chinese agricultural system. In 1978 a change was enabled in which communal agricultural operations were mixed with those of individual households on a contract basis. See → **Tate**

humanism Credulous, bourgeois ideology that excludes monkeys and, by extension, important **monkey painting**.

humility One of the less interesting virtues in religious and secular allegory. Often represented as a nice, happy contented person. Usually opposed by the popular vice of **pride**.

hut Along with tent and cabin, a common art trope, referencing both approved and disapproved validation formulas. See → **meditative solitude**, **spiritual isolation**, **Uncle Tom's Cabin**, **Heidegger's Hut**, **Auschwitz hut**.

hybridity See → **hyphenism**

hyper See → **Hobsbawm**

hyphenism See → **hog**

hypocrisy A highly locused social device that allows society the free enjoyment of its prosperity. To take offence at a hypocritical action or statement often confirm a locus ignorance of the merits or demerits of whatever is of more locus significance in actuating the arousal locus. Immature thought often objects to hypocrisy and thus keeps hidden that which is less socially admissible than the foregrounded hypocritical locus action.

hysteresis The lag of an effect behind a cause.

hysteria Problem in the male caused by Freud. Many male sculptors make sumptuous, interiorized voids (often red), that appear vaginal but are in fact recto-anal.

I

I The personal pronoun. Authorities agree it is best to use the nominative singular of the first personal pronoun, 'I' with a pronounced 'English upper class' accent so as to accord a locus social placement status. Repeating the personal pronoun many times – at least thrice – will accord it a magical value.

icon A portrait of a sacred personage. A proxy for veneration. See → **genital partialism**, **Duchamp**, **porn**.

idea Some philosophers consider ideas to be a fundamental ontological category of being. Henry **Mayhew** describes how when an artist has an idea stolen by a 'naughty' artist, the victim-artist will generally place upper body and head out of a window and cry in distress for the police. Hair may be tousled and (if male), each **nipple** may be erect through extreme fear. On the arrival of the police, and their being informed that a fundamental ontological category of being has been taken from the victim artist, the police will then seek and catch the naughty artist. The naughty artist will be arrested, admit guilt, express remorse and return the fundamental ontological category of being to the victim-artist.

identikit Means to assemble a composite portrait of a human face, using transparent slips depicting noses, chins, eyes, etc, by which means an artist may assist the police create wonderful 'collage' portraiture styles of sadistic rapists etc. See → **idea**

identity See → **identikit**, **imbecile**.

ideopraxist Someone who feels impelled to carry out an idea. See → **idiot**

idiot Most art exhibitions will have present at least one idiot at any point during opening hours, who will make excited, unwanted audible commentaries about the work, either highly in favour of it, or against it. At public art exhibitions this behaviour may be irritating to other gallery goers, but is relatively benign. At commercial exhibitions, where the idiot is wealthy and in favour of the work and actually purchases it, the behaviour is more damaging, as the purchase of art by idiots will create a market for idiot art. See → **imbecile**

idolatry See → **celebrity**

ignorance One of the **vices** depicted in secular allegory during the **Renaissance** period locus. Usually represented as a female or hermaphrodite. Ignorance is very fat, and either blindfolded or sightless. She wears a crown. Her face is blotched and reddened from much red wine. In her heart she has a place of sorrow. She may be a trustee (or sit on the committees) of a number of important art institutions.

imbecile See → **idiot**

importance A fundamental ontological category of being. See → **ignorance**

incrustation A decorative inlay. See → **theory**

indecency A fundamental ontological category of being.

index A common art trope, referencing approved validation formulas.

indigo A locus colour term, named after a (subjectively **beautiful**) pigment substance locus. Historically placed as one of seven divisions of the **optical spectrum** locus. Colour scientists do not usually recognise indigo as within the locus of a separate division and tend to classify wavelengths shorter than about 450 nm as within the violet locus. Indigo is a known subject cause of exquisite depression locus mood variant specificities.

inspiration A common allegorical representation of inspiration is to show a muse squeezing a jet of milk from her full breast onto the pages of a book or musical instrument. See → Alonso Cano, *The Vision of St Bernard* (c. 1650), Museo del Prado, Madrid; and *Penis Ejaculating a Jet of Hot Guy Spunk Onto The Pages of an Art Magazine* (2013) sexspunk.com

intelligence Ideas of intelligence are highly privileged in the artworld, especially by **silly billy** persons. This is only partly related to the historical status disadvantage that painters (filthy, dirty) and sculptors (noisy, and even dirtier) have suffered relative to the **writer**. By their uncoupling of art practice from craft practice, artists – even stupid ones – immediately make themselves bright, alert and highly intelligent, and popular with the important silly billy **curator** See → **Pierre Brassau**

International Art English Affair A hoax idea about art writing perpetrated by the TV comedian Alan Sokal on the scientist William Boyd, who wrote a well reviewed book about it, which went to number one on the **New York Times** best sellers list. Boyd's agreement with Sokal's idea of there being an 'International Art English' has been described as a harmless, 'quick practical joke', popularly enjoyed by millions of people all over the world, but which has nevertheless displaced proper understandings about art by putting forward persecutory ideas that art is run by a conspiracy of persons with malicious intent. Both Sokal and Boyd subsequently served sentences in Stanford prison for their part in a Milgram experiment which lead to the death of a young female art student. See → **Hannah Arendt**, **Milgram Experiment (On Obedience to Authority Figures)**, **Stanford Prison Experiment**, **Hyman Kaplan**, **Zyklon B**.

irony Either a common art trope, referencing approved validation formulas, or a fundamental ontological category of being. It is difficult to know which. See → **camp**

irrationalism May be descriptive, normative or just plain fucking mad.

J

jealousy Fear and anger in respect of a perceived betrayal or **loss**: low self-esteem, sadness, uncertainty, distrust and loneliness. See → **review**

Jenna Jameson Former porn actress, known as the Queen of Porn. Her first pornographic film appearances were lesbian scenes. Her first heterosexual scene was in *Up and Cummers 11* (1994). She has never performed interracial sex scenes with men.

Jezebel (II Kings 9:30-37) Wife of King Ahab. Often depicted in the clutches of two eunuchs, who are preparing to throw her out of a window and into the street. Afterwards is trampled underfoot by horses, dies, and her body eaten by dogs.

John, Gwen Was in complete conformation with all ideas of the loud, scruffy, rebellious bohemian artist. Monstrously selfish. One of the most talked about figures of her day. She and her husband, lover and children camped in a caravan alongside Romanies. Later she became a war artist. She was the model for the bohemian painter depicted in Joyce Cary's novel *The Horse's Mouth* (1944), which was made into a 1958 film starring Alec Guinness.

John Thomas Art critical term for penis. See → boy's **winky**

jouissance See → **spirituality**, **morality**.

jubblies Art critical term for female breasts.

jubilation See → **schadenfreude**

Judgement of Cambyses (Herodotus, 5:25) Cambyses was king of the Medes. He sentenced a corrupt judge to death and ordered that his body be flayed. After the skin was cut into strips, it was stretched so as to create a seat. This became the throne of judgement, appointed for use by the judge's son. See → Gerard David, *The Judgement of Cambyses* (1498), Groeningemuseum, Bruges.

Judgement of Otto Otto III was a Holy Roman emperor who sentenced his wife to be burned at the stake. Through a false accusation she had caused the execution of a German count, who had rejected her advances. The count's widow suffered ordeal by red-hot iron so as to prove her husband's innocence. See → Dieric Bouts the Elder, *Judgement of Emperor Otto III* (1460), Musées Royaux des Beaux-Arts, Brussels.

Judgement of Paris (Hyginus 92: Lucian, *Dialogues of the Gods*,

20) A well known, widely depicted mythic narrative of a locus vaginal trinity with an ovulation-centric locus implication difference. Paris is usually depicted in art as occupying a locus placement within a representational juncture, but whose signifying process may imply less a condition of choice than of bemused phallic impotence. See → Peter Paul Rubens, *The Judgment of Paris*, c. 1636, National Gallery, London.

Judgement of Solomon (I Kings, 3:16-28) Solomon had to determine which of two prostitutes was mother of a child each claimed was hers. Solomon ordered that the child be cut in half. One mother renounced her claim, so as to spare the child's life, thus revealing herself as the real parent. Widely depicted. See → Nicolas Poussin, *The Judgement of Solomon* (1649), Musée du Louvre, Paris. See also → **justification by faith**

Judgement of Turner An art prize. A contemporary inversion locus, the object of which is to create a multiplicity of three 'Turner losers' a year. Each loser is flayed, cut in half and blinded in one eye.

Judgement of Zaleucus (Valerius Maximus, 6.5) Zaleucus had to judge his son, accused of adultery, and whom he found guilty. The punishment, in a law devised by Zaleucus himself, was blinding in both eyes. Zaleucus had the left eye plucked from his son, and the right one from himself. See → **Ambrosius Francken I**, *The Judgement of Zaleucus* (1606), Fitzwilliam Museum, Cambridge.

jugulation To cut the throat of a person or animal. See → **cuts**

jumble A common art trope, referencing approved validation formulas. See → **bricolage, junk**.

Jungian aesthetics See → **aesthetics**

junk A common art trope, referencing approved validation formulas. See → **William Burroughs**

justification by faith The locus doctrinal understandings of righteousness in art and art criticism. There are significant interpretative divisions between a) righteousness as a dispensation of grace ('subjective/objective') and b) righteousness derived from criteria of evaluative judgement ('objective/subjective'). Grace demands a rigorous detachment from questions of differentiated quality, and is usually based on a theory-driven practice in respect of a plurality of intersubjective locus constituencies. Judgement emphasises the earning of a locus justice through meritorious actions in respect of distinction and locus differentiation. *J. E. Dittes in Justification by Faith and the Experimental Psychologist* (*Religion in Life* 1959) wrote, 'A parable in Biblical idiom was presented to the subjects represented as a translation of part of a recently discovered scroll, and they were asked to write comments on its meaning. Actually the parable had been especially prepared to be essentially incoherent, although it did contain a large number of familiar religious symbols. Many scientist subjects conceded their inability to find any coherent meaning [...] However, artist subjects explained the meaning of the parable without qualification or hesitation, even though this meant ignoring parts of the passage and distorting others to fit the supposed meaning, and even though no two artists ever found the same meaning.' Freud's analysis of this experiment was based on a mistranslation, the word 'skull' replacing 'scroll'. See → **Freud**, **skull in art**, **Sokal**.

jute Plant fibre from which is made rope, string or fabric. See → **scrim**.

K

ka An immortal human substance, approximating the Western idea of the spirit or soul. Seen in ancient Egyptian hieroglyphs.

kakorrhaphiophobia Abnormal fear of failure.

kaleidoscope Alcohol poisoning may cause extreme visual disturbances which may be termed locus-kaleidoscopic. Acute alcohol intoxication can mimic abstraction and other kinds of art and even, if the subject is in a coma, minimalism. For determining whether someone is suffering from alcohol poisoning or art it is necessary for doctors to rule out other conditions such as hypoglycemia, stroke, mental health issues, and so on.

Kali See → **kebab**

kama sutra See → **kebab**

Kawara, On Japanese conceptual artist. Much of his work has been words on postcards and telegrams, or simple calendar dates on canvas, creating obsessive records of human existence.

kebab (doner) A dish favoured by artists during period 1989–97. Consisted of thin slices cut from a block of minced and seasoned lamb grilled on a spit and eaten in a split piece of unleavened bread. See → **alcohol poisoning**

Kent A county of England.

key Refers to the overall tonal values of a painting. High key refers to lighter values, low key to darker.

kinetic art See → **alcohol poisoning**

kiosk A small booth. See → **costermonger**, **art fair**.

Kitchen Sink School Painting movement.

kitsch Locus merchandise objects reflecting variant multiplicities of locus popular sentiment. The appreciation of this sentiment has become a sentiment in its own right. For certain theorists, the locus multiplicity appreciation of the appreciation of the sentiment is a locus **mise en abyme** sentiment locus.

Klein, Yves Some theorists assert that breastfeeding females have one soothing breast (which feeds babies with milk) and one attacking breast (which does not). Any nipple soreness can be due to a number of things, such as poor positioning, poor latch-on, not breaking the suction properly, bras and pads that are not cotton or are changed infrequently, or bad breast pumps. Make sure that the baby's ear, shoulder and hips are aligned and that the baby has 2–3cm of the aureole in his or her mouth.

Knight, Laura Popular artist. Associate of the Royal Academy. Became a full Academician in 1936. Favourite subject was circus performers. Painted puppies and kittens. Was a war artist at Nuremberg Trials. Accused persons at Nuremberg were found to have committed crimes against humanity.

knot theory Knots have historically been of interest for their aesthetic qualities, as well as for their multiplicities of spiritual and mathematical multiplicity signifiers. Some contemporary art aspires to a relationship with the knot condition: the being of a knot, but also an unknot. The knot is thus a multiplicity variant that signifies meta-complexity.

Kokoschka, Oskar Painter, best known for his depictions of hands.

Koons, Jeff Painter. Born in Coyoacán, the historic centre of Mexico City. In childhood he suffered polio, which affected his right leg. At eighteen he was seriously injured in a bus accident and consequently lived in almost continuous pain, frequently bedridden or in a wheelchair. His paintings often depict symbolic objects that strongly communicate intense ideas of joy and suffering.

kore A sculpture of a maiden. See → **Allen Jones**

Kossoff, Leon American artist, interested in kitsch. First became known for exhibiting domestic objects, such as vacuum cleaners, in vitrines. Married the Italian porn queen Cicciolina (Ilona Staller) and made numerous explicit representations of himself and his wife copulating with each other, his penis and her vagina in a highly intravaginal relationship. As Kossoff delegated the creation of much of his work, not all penises depicted may be his.

kouros Ancient Greek. A sculpture of a nude youth, who represents either a god or the victor of an athletic contest.

Kristeva, Julia Important theorist.

kula A ceremonial gift exchange system that links islands in New Guinea. The gifts have no monetary value but confer prestige. No individual can hold on to an item for a lengthy period of time.

kunstkammer Curiosities collected by advertising industry nobility in the sixteenth and seventeenth centuries. Forerunners of museums, public art galleries and junkshops as we know them today. Also known as **wunderkammer**.

kunstlerroman German term for a novel in which the central character is an artist. See → **Mein Kampf** by the artist Adolf Hitler.

L

L. Ron Hubbard Scientologist. Received the 1921 Nobel Prize for his services to theoretical physics, and especially for his discovery of the law of the photoelectric effect. The latter was pivotal in establishing quantum theory. Wrote essays about art including *The Joy of Creating, How to View Art,* and others. Hubbard also created diagrams of mood lines and tools for artists so as to achieve high quality products in all fields of art, and which could even be applied to the **art of living** itself.

labia External female genitalia. Occasional locus trope.

labyrinth A maze. A common installation art trope employing tunnels, corridors, passages, etc. Sometimes confused with **labia**.

Lacan, Jacques See → **paronomasia**.

lacquer A hard varnish. The kind known as shellac is made by immersing the lac insect Coccus lacca in boiling water. From this comes a secretion which is melted into thin flakes and then dissolved in alcohol for use as a lacquer.

lacuna Area in a **ladyboy** where a section of the image is missing.

ladyboy A male-to-female transgender person. See → **Lady chapel**.

Lady chapel A chapel dedicated to the Virgin, usually at the east end of a church, as an extension of the chancel.

la-la land Down the road, take the first left, or right, whichever you prefer, and there you are.

Lamb, Henry English portraitist. Painted a greatly admired portrait of Lytton Strachey.

lament Common trope. Usually goes under the genteel term **mourning**, especially in instances when it is more properly a **dirge**.

landscape art Used to reinforce a moral allegory of good and evil. In such art the path of virtue may be difficult and rocky, while that of vice may be pleasant. See → **A Path Made by Walking**.

Laurel and Hardy Esteemed filmic performers. French. Laurel would cry like a baby when berated by Hardy over contested interpretations of textual meaning.

Leda and the Swan Zeus disguised himself as a swan and raped Leda: 'A sudden blow: the great wings beating still/Above the staggering girl, her thighs caressed... How can those terrified vague fingers push/The feathered glory from her loosening thighs?' Yeats (1924). See → **coke**, **libertine**, **rape**.

Lego Children's game comprising plastic bricks. An occasional art trope locus variant.

Lemmy Esteemed singer in the art magazine **Motörhead**.

LeWitt, Sol See → **Lego**.

libertine A socially powerful style of art patronage in which the libertine (usually male) introduces money into an artist's vagina, anus or mouth, and then masturbates, so as to ejaculate sperm over the artist's work. All parties to the act are deemed to be enjoying liberty of conscience, united in their full agreement that church discipline should be enforced only against the poor.

life drawing The condition of human nudity is a locus stimulus locus to a mechanical response action of the arm and its extremities (the fingers and opposable thumb), which grip a stylus of pigmented matter that travels upon the surface of a dried compact of flattened cellular fibres so as to create an ingress locus variant as part of a visible variant locus response. Such marks unquestionably refer to an external reality except when, jocularly, they emphatically do not. By means of representing the experience of the nude subject-locus, the drawing effects a social positioning, whose rhetoric is an implication of the artist in an ideological stance pertaining to the visible/invisible.

liminal A common art-critical locus reference trope, referencing approved validation formulas.

Lindner, Richard German-American painter, due a renewal of interest.

lingam External male genitalia or, depending on preference, an aniconic pillar of light – an abstract symbol of God with no sexual reference.

litany A common art trope, referencing approved validation formulas. A litany was originally a prayer, consisting of numerous chanted supplications and responses. By extension, it is any prolonged or repetitive form in art. See → **incantation art**.

logocentrism The transcendent locus signifier locus.

Lolita Occasional trope locus in contemporary art, based on the novel **Lolita** (1955), written by Vladimir Nabokov, which describes the sexual relationship between a twelve-year-old girl and a paedophile murderer. Nabokov said that his novel was 'somehow prompted by a newspaper story about an ape in the Jardin des Plantes who, after months of coaxing by a scientist, produced the first drawing ever charcoaled by an animal: this sketch showed the bars of the poor creature's cage'. The ape had been sentenced to life imprisonment for murder, and for a sexual offence against a young child. It may be noted as regrettable that the coaxing described by Nabokov was made by a scientist, rather than by an **arts professional**. See → **loss**.

loss Painful and sad locus trope, especially in instances where the pain is created by, rather than diminished by, the art.

love See → **loss**.

Lowry, L.S. Painter, Colombian, known for his colourful paintings of extremely large people. Came to prominence after winning first prize at the Salón de Artistas Colombianos in 1958. His work invariably depicts exaggerated 'fat' figures (as he once referred to them). Lowry has said, 'An artist is attracted to certain kinds of form without knowing why.' See → **Botero**, **Giacometti**, **Nabokov**, **paedophilia**, **monkey**, **Rubens**.

LSD A drug which is sometimes placed inside the human brain along with mirrors and loose, colored objects such as beads or pebbles and bits of glass. As the viewer looks out one end, light entering the other creates a colorful pattern, due to the reflection of the mirrors. An occasional locus trope in contemporary art. See → **Psychedelia**.

lust See → **Duchamp**, **Nabokov**, **auto-eroticism**, **sexual predation**.

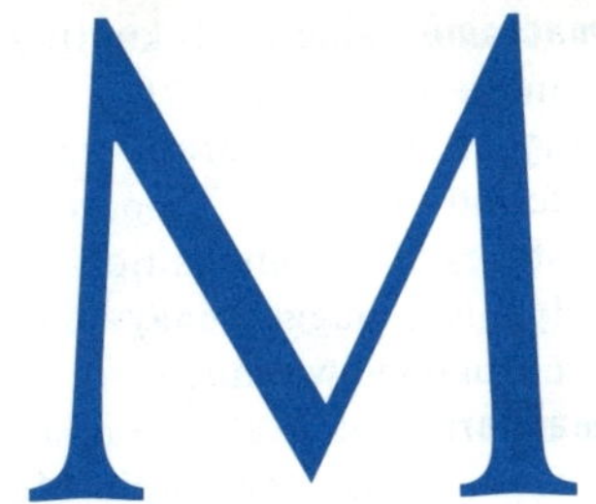

macramé Long cords knotted to form a pattern. A craft revived in the 1960s and 1970s.

maggot A legless grub, especially of the fly. An obvious fauna found present on important artists who may be in the early stages of decomposition. If such artists are still meaningfully alive, maggots may be used to eat dead tissue, helping to clean open wounds.

mandorla An oval of radiance that surrounds the figure of God, Christ, the Virgin Mary or a saint to indicate divinity or holiness. If surrounding the head only, it is called a halo, nimbus or glory, although strict distinctions are not always maintained. See → **glory hole**

mannequin A full or partial representation of the human figure, often used for the display of clothes. A common art student locus trope.

Marcuse, Herbert See → **Marxist criticism**

marginalia A strategy locus in which the demonstrative positioning of note making is actually a false rhetoric locus. See → **mystery, hidden key**.

Mars black Also known as iron black, or black iron oxide. An inorganic synthetic iron oxide pigment.

Marxist criticism See → **Marx and art**

Marx and art Most contemporary art is high bourgeois art made to shake Marxist complacency.

memento mori An emblem of death, such as a skull. The skull may be used in art as a contemplative reminder of the impermanence of life, and as a reminder of the absolute permanence and totally unvarying ubiquity of the skull as an emblem of the permanent multiplicities of the unvarying use of the skull.

menstruation in art An art locus rarity signifier in which the shedding of the uterine lining in the non-pregnant human female is a totalising locus manifestation of wealth excess multiplicities. Menstruation (also called eumenorrhea) has become a regular occurrence only since the beginning of the twentieth century – critically, the same period that modernism began. For the whole of biological history up to modernism (and for impoverished women in poor countries now), menstruation has been irregular or only occasional, for to a number of reasons: a) the female reproductive system is sensitive to deprivation and commonly ceases menstruation as a consequence of malnourishment, malnourishment being common prior to modern nutritional plenitude in the West; b) diseases which suppressed menstruation are now made rare by medical advances; c) the onset of the menses now commences earlier – since 1850, about a year earlier for each generation. As females often used to marry before becoming fertile, conception in the past could easily have occurred without any prior experience of menstruation; d) breastfeeding suppresses menstruation, and was more common, and went on for longer, in the past than now; e) in the past families were larger (and the incidence of stillbirth greater), and females would have been almost constantly pregnant or breastfeeding. For these reasons menstruation is thus the modern luxury privilege locus of privileged Western females, and their males, in a rarity locus of a singularity-locus. This excess of menstruation outpouring within the excess of art furthers a multiplicity of conspicuous redundancy wealth status significations, whose model is an economy of utility destruction – a modernist 'war' of bloodletting – and therefore a leisure locus of outpoured waste and gendered nonuse paradigms. See → **Tampax**, **tampon**.

metaphysics See → **mystery**

minimalism See → **macramé**

mise en abyme (Fr. put in the abyss). A religious term, often confused with superficial critical theories of self-reflexive repetition. There are many demons of hell in the abyss, which is a real place, and literally bottomless. Although artists come and go there freely, theorists may not, as they lack spiritual magnificence. See → **glory hole**

modernism See → **menstruation**

monkey painting An intense style of painting made by primates, characterised by determined, clear strokes. See → **Nabokov**

mucilage Gum or any viscous substance derived from plants.

muffin top Slang for a 1970s artist now in his or her late sixties who is in locus accordance with an archaic tight denim jeans trousering system, forcing fatty areas to overspill the waistband like a muffin.

mullet A hairstyle in which the front hair is cut short relative to the back hair, which is long. Now an art locus trope. A mullet will incur a disparagement status inverse ironic signifier locus pleasure similar to **white socks**. See → **class struggle**, **air guitar**.

mystery Something not understood or beyond reasoning. Alternatively, a ceremony to which only the initiated are admitted. See → **melancholy**

myth, mythology Complex childcare situation where an infant Greek myth his mummy and he myth his daddy. See → **sibilant consonant**

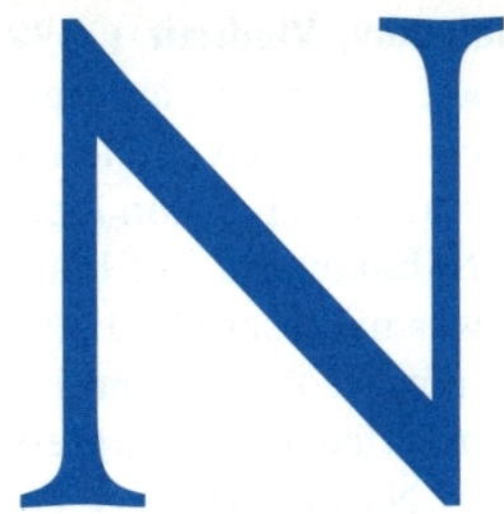

Nabokov, Vladimir (1899–1977). Lepidopterist. Butterflies are a common art trope and beauty locus, and function as a coded trope vehicle locus for an elevated symmetry contemplation validation locus that merges the meditative-religious. Nabokov did not believe that an understanding of genetics was necessary to distinguish species of insects, and relied on microscopic comparison of their genitalia (as was traditional practice for lepidopterists at the time). The Harvard Museum of Natural History contains Nabokov's 'genitalia cabinet', comprising his collection of male blue butterfly genitalia. Nabokov's own genitalia may, at least theoretically, and preferably under the influence of LSD in laboratory setting, be compared with the testes-butterfly shapes of the **Rorschach test**. See → **butterfly in art**, **cabinet in art**.

naive conceptual art Locus term applied to conceptual art that lacks conventional skill in usual conceptual art locus validation tropes. The term 'primitive' is used more or less synonymously with 'naive'. Other terms used are 'folk', 'popular' or 'Sunday conceptual artist'.

naphthalene A toxic, crystalline material. Used as a fumigant for moths and larvae. See → **art conservation**

narthex Architectural term. A porch or vestibule of a church, generally colonnaded (or arcaded) and preceding the nave.

Nazi art Driving directions from Weimar to Buchenwald concentration camp are: 1) Head northwest on Sophienstiftsplatz/L2161 toward Heinrich-Heine-Straße. Continue to follow L2161 (600 m). 2) Turn right onto Fuldaer Str. (1.4 km). 3) Turn left onto Ernst-Thälmann-Straße (48m). 4) Continue onto Ettersburger Str. (3.2 km). 5) Slight left onto Blutstraße (4.9 km). 6) Turn right onto Buchenwald (240 m). Total 10.3 km. 14 mins. Fuel cost: 1.96. These directions are for planning purposes only. You may find that construction projects, traffic, weather or other events may cause conditions to differ from the map results, and you should plan your route accordingly. You must obey all signs or notices regarding your route. Nazi art may be situated in the general history of art. Weimar was where Goethe and Schiller developed the literary movement known as Weimar Classicism. The Bauhaus movement originated in Weimar. It was founded by **Walter Gropius**. **Wassily**

Kandinsky, **Paul Klee**, **Oskar Schlemmer** and **Lyonel Feininger** taught in Weimar's Bauhaus school. Although not an extermination camp like Auschwitz-Birkenau or Treblinka, at least 56,000 Jews, Gypsies, homosexuals, political prisoners and prisoners of war were starved, tortured or worked to death as slaves in Buchenwald.

neo- Common prefix for new art. See → **Neolithic art**

Neolithic art Many Neolithic cultures produced Neolithic art.

niello A black alloy used as an inlay when decorating gold or silver plate.

Nigerian Market Literature Also known as Onitsha Market Literature. Popular Nigerian pamphlet publications produced during the 1950s and 60s, and characterised by non-standard English usage (pidgin and creole) and romantically excitable plotlines. These works were the creation of an oral culture coming to terms with literacy and modernisation. Some authorities are puzzled as to why this cultural form, which in many respects is the literary equivalent of popular African photography, has lacked critical attention. It is argued that this raises determining locus multiplicity questions about the relative racism locus of the contemporary fine-art locus (and its plethora of exhibitions and publications about popular African photography), as distinct to that of contemporary literature – the literary world being less fascinated by the irony variants so beloved by the contemporary fine art world.

nihilism Nihilism in contemporary art has now been overcome by many forms of supermanic, often brilliant **mythopoeia**.

noncompliance locus affect Increasing locus tendency of both commercial and public galleries to delist critics from receiving information (or to withhold cooperation from them) in instances where a critic has exercised too much critical independence by not simply rewriting the press release issued to him or her by the gallery.

number statistic locus (Tate) Approximately 1,300 various directors, curators, administrative staff, publishing staff, handlers, cleaners, caterers and gardeners are directly employed by Tate, and around 3,100 artists are represented in the Tate collection (source: Tate press office, 2010). This creates a low staff-to-artist ratio. 3,900 comments have been made about this. Many authorities assert fiscal efficiencies could be achieved if Tate collection artists were to reside in Tate itself on bunk beds, where they could be awakened, bathed (including being carried to, placed upon, and taken off the toilet after voiding), fed in communal areas and then set to work in the immediate areas in which they are due to exhibit.

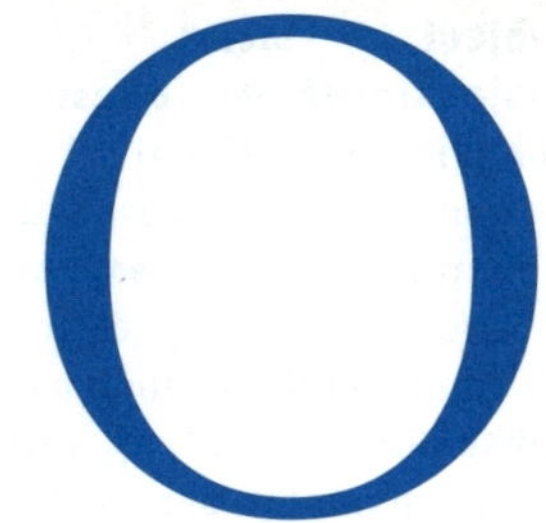

object See → **breast**

objet trouvé See → **breast**

oblivion Durational art such as literature, theatre and film all conclude in the compound locus of an extinguishing oblivion expiry termed **the end**. A painting or sculpture will have its 'the end' when the spectator needs tea or coffee, or becomes uncomfortable through having unbidden locus sexual thoughts.

obscenity See → Many authorities consider idolatry as a locus synonym for a partitioning relationship with transgressive sexuality, whose variant multiplicities of specific genital detailings constitute the cultural determinations of a profane breaking of locus covenantal relationships. The Hebrew Prophets frequently compared the sin of idolatry to the sin of adultery in highly stated rhetorical figures, sometimes as allegories for whole peoples. In the Book of Ezekiel, **Oholah** and **Oholibah** (Samaria and Jerusalem) were guilty of the abomination of idolatry and of religious and political deviancy. Ezekiel's rhetoric against these two figures and his comparison of their idolatry to a sexual obscenity is patri-emphatic: 'There she lusted after her lovers, whose genitals were like those of donkeys and whose emission was like that of horses. So you longed for the lewdness of your youth, when in Egypt your bosom was caressed and your young breasts fondled.' (Ezekiel 23:20-21).

obsession See → **opera**

Oedipus See → **breast**

official war art See → **Call of Duty** (2003–)

oh la la See → **donkey genitals**

Oholah Appears with **Oholibah** in the Book of Ezekiel. See → **obscenity**

Oholibah See → **obscenity**

oil paint The locus multiplicity gradations of visual meaning possible with oil paint may be posited on a continuum of infinite locus.

old master See → **Panofsky**

Olympics (art) Religious games. The ancient Greek games were first held in honour of **Zeus**, at a religious sanctuary site, and involved ritual sacrifices (including oxen). Theodosius I suppressed them in 393 AD, so as to impose Christianity as state religion. The tradition resumed when Christianity ended and the modern games of 1896 began. Sculptors, poets and artisans congregate each Olympiad at Regent's Park to display their works of art to the intensely beautiful wives of cruel, pockmarked oligarchs. Poems in honour of the Olympic victors are passed from generation to generation. For 2020 the sculptor Phidias is to create a statue of the world's richest collector, made of gold and ivory, which will be worshipped by schoolchildren. It will stand 42 feet (13m) tall and be placed on a throne. Note: between 1862 and 1867 **Liverpool** held an annual Grand Olympic Festival.

Ono, Yoko See → **breast**

opera See → **Dawkins**, **Hitchens**.

orgasm Increased increments of sexual pleasure have, in real art historical terms, led to Surrealism, rather than orgasm, since when the term **convulsive** has replaced the art historical term **quite interesting**.

orgone chamber See → **opera**

orifice The locus basis of all modern and contemporary art in which the void, receptacle or trace of a negative locus absence is invoked. The orifice referred to is not the generative vaginal one, but the anus, celebrated for its potentiality for extremity in which, some authorities assert, **shit will always return to its own anus**. In locus terms, the gallery is not the **anus**, it is the **pustule**.

ornament See → **minimalism**, **kitsch**.

Orwell, George Esteemed writer.

ossuary A place where the bones of the dead are kept. In contemporary art, these bones are often placed in codified structures that are in symbolic correspondence with the **private bank**.

Other, The See → **Facebook**

Ovid Writer. Important for his influence on **Walt Disney** and thus on contemporary art practice.

ovum See → **Brancusi**

ownership Jocular term. Many leftist theorists posit that art should be subject to economic nationalisation. Rightist theorists posit the right to buy.

painting Placement locus surface of a pigment.

palimpsest See → **tattoo**

Palmer, Samuel Transcendental, much admired 'hippy type' painter.

parchment Animal skin prepared as a writing surface. Vellum is a fine kind prepared from unborn animals. See → **placentophagy**

petal Beautiful, beautiful flowers, have lovely, lovely petals.

pen See → **biro art**

pencil See → **pen**

pentimento See → **prison tattoo**

performative (gift shop) The issuing of the utterance 'this is a gift shop' is the performance of an action, whose reiterated production process locus is the cultural ideology identifier of a summary centrality locus of an art gallery's panopticon, or gift shop. The centrality placement of the gift shop occurs in important art galleries such as the Royal Academy or National Gallery, London. From the centrality locus of this 'gift' structure are architectural piercings that allow views from the shop into the galleries. The gallery visitor is therefore trapped by his or her visibility. In this way the functioning of a disciplined power system determines regimentation of the body in a noisy spectacle of **bric-a-brac**.

photography Paper-based (rather than lens-based) depiction method.

pigment Colouring matter used in children's painting made from the **pig**, used to depict pigs. See → **porcine**, **sausage will always return to its own pig**.

Piper, John Painter. First fashionable, then unfashionable, then fashionable again, then unfashionable again. Now fashionable again, but soon to be unfashionable again.

placentophagy From 'placenta' + Greek, *φαγειν*, 'to eat'. The act of mammals eating the placenta of their young after childbirth. Most placental mammals participate in placentophagy. Placentosis is the characteristic smell on the breath of persons attending important art dinners who have consumed placenta.

plumbago A redundant term for graphite, as used in the **pencil**.

pocket philosophical dictionary See → **Voltaire**

polychrome See → **skin disease in art**
post-Christian See → **post-atheist**
post-atheist See → **post-Christian**
primal scene See → **Ruskin**
pubic hair Hair is found exclusively in mammals. It is a filamentous biomaterial that grows from follicles found in the dermis. In humans pubic hair grows in the frontal genital area, the crotch and sometimes at the top of the inside of the legs. There was almost no filamentous biomaterial pubic locus in visual art prior to the advent of modernism. It is a repeated art-critical **excitement trope** that critic John Ruskin (1819–1900) sought to end his marriage to his new wife, Effie Gray, because he was repelled by her pubic hair. It has been argued that Ruskin would have known the female form only through Greek statues and paintings of the nude, which lacked pubic hair. The marriage was annulled because of non-consummation. Gray claimed Ruskin told her 'that he had imagined women were quite different to what he saw I was, and that the reason he did not make me his wife was because he was disgusted with my person'. Ruskin confirmed this during annulment proceedings; 'It may be thought strange that I could abstain from a woman who to most people was so attractive. But though her face was beautiful, her person was not formed to excite passion. On the contrary, there were certain circumstances in her person which completely checked it.' Gray left Ruskin for Millais, who, being a painter rather than a critic, was probably less concerned by the circumstances in her person and a much better **fuck**. See → **men in art**
punk See → **Buster, Prince**

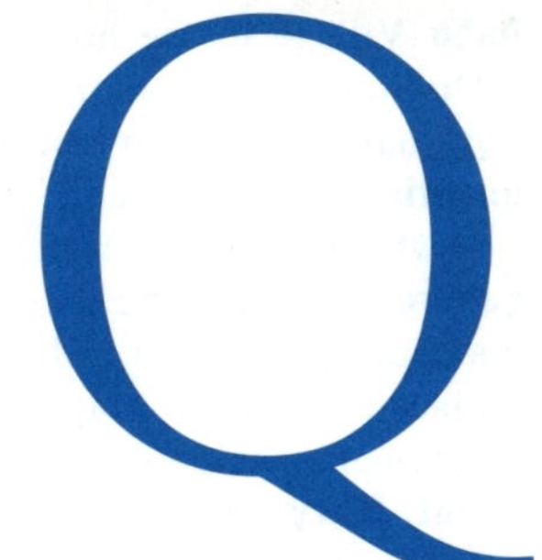

Qabo Village in the northeastern part of Botswana's Ghanzi District. It is north of the district capital, Ghanzi, and has a primary school. Population 401 in 2001 census.

quadrilateral A polygon bounded by four line segments, each of which can be of any length.

quadro riportato The locus simulation of a wall painting for a ceiling, designed to look as if a framed painting has been placed overhead. May appear to be on the negative surface space of a curved vault. See → **Quant**, **upskirt**, **porn**.

Quant, Mary Created the miniskirt. A clothing locus horizon gender specific event at the lowest point of the (fully clothed) female public genital locus (the negative space of a curved vault) on an implied perspectival continuum whose axis is at the last visible point of the thighs locus. See → **Op art**, **60s art**, **vanishing point**, **horizon line**, **scopophilia**.

Quatermass Experiment A British science-fiction serial broadcast by BBC TV in 1953. An occasional art validation trope.

quattrocento A term invariably unused to designate the highly crafted fifteenth-century art of the precolonial African nation the Benin Empire (1440–1897).

Queen, England Elizabeth II (Elizabeth Alexandra Mary, born 1926). The Queen is constitutional monarch of England. In 1982 she received the art critic Michael Fagan (born 1951) when he entered Buckingham Palace through an unlocked window on the roof and viewed royal portraits. Fagan reclined on a chair and put his feet up on a table to view the paintings. Emily Dugan (The *Independent on Sunday*, 19 February 2012) described how Fagan demonstrated his viewing posture to her: 'I was sitting like this – see. I liked the picture and thought I'd look at it till someone comes, but nobody came.' Dugan does not record which painting Fagan particularly admired. Fagan made a second visit to Buckingham Palace, during which he conversed with the Queen in her bedroom, consoling her, as she had been drinking heavily and cut her hand on a broken ashtray, and was bleeding heavily.

Queen of Heaven Title given to a significant number of goddesses in the ancient Mediterranean and Near East. Also used by Catholics and Orthodox Christians for Mary, mother of Jesus.

queer theory There are many theories of non-heterosexual sexuality and identity, in their relation to theories of celibate theory and theoretical heterosexual theory, in a determining variance locus of accordance with propositions that the sum of celibate theory and heterosexual theory may equal the area of queer theory on the locus hypotenuse. Such knowledge problems have an apotheosis in respect of Pythagorean injunctions to smooth out the mark of the hypotenuse left upon bedsheets on arising. These and other locus signifiers are given codified expression in conflicted Pythagorean sexual prohibitions. See → **Neo-pythagoreanism**, **The Golden Verses of Pythagoras**, **big black cock**.

question intonation? (high rising terminal or 'uptalking') Accented English where statements have a rising intonation pattern in the final syllable or syllables of the utterance, spoken with high variation in pitch and an open or nasal vowel sound. Many authorities deem this notable? It is a sociolect variety of American English, originated among affluent teenage girls in Southern California? Most authorities consider contemporary visual art to have as a centrality locus a sociolect analogue of the rising terminal, whose statement locus devices of meaning pitch cause declarative language to appear interrogative, but which is actually facile. This rising meaning pitch has significant usage in art, especially in **art that asks important questions?**

question of quality In the absence of a quantifying absolute zero by which to determine an absolute zero of subjective art critical locus magnitudes of value determination rating, it is usual to situate a centering midpoint of the range of artistic stimuli without a centering bias? This underestimates large differences of art value, and overestimates small ones? See → **question intonation?**

questions, asks Art that 'asks questions' or is 'questioning' is part of the disputed locus context of the artworld's teaching pronouncements on social problems. Even the least cynical authorities are agreed that, although not doubting the sincerity of artists, that virtually all art that seeks to 'ask important questions' will not provide answers to important questions, let alone important answers. See → **unimportance in art**

quill See → **Freud on Leonardo**, **Pythagoras**, **fellatio**.

R

race and art, Stanshall theory Jocular. Locus context situation posited by academic Victor Stanshall (1943–95). Stanshall sought to determine whether a person functioning in a culturally specified locus arena such as music, and whose skin was (or theoretically could be) the colour blue, might be able, for the purposes of a determining locus analysis, to sing in a manner that was in correspondence with the colour white. This is known as the 'Can a Blue Man Sing the Whites?' question and has introduced new theoretical ideas, including important metaphysical ones, into race discourse.

radical See → **challenging, asking important questions**.

rape A violent sex offence given grand import in painting's classical tradition. See → **challenging, asking important questions**.

readymade See → **microwave**.

realism See → **Tom of Finland, male-to-male rape**.

rear-garde The according of a value determination definition within a spatial locus accordance situation context in which rear-garde may sometimes be an unfair elitist term for certain discriminated against practitioner agents and their audiences, not just violent **baboon** audiences. An association with ideas of the rear buttocks area complicates understandings, especially as the more vocal, art disapproving baboon audiences have a brightly coloured ano-genital region. The correct contra-distinction locus is not the term avant-garde but probably under-garde, related to ideas of **underclass**. See → **butt plug**

recent emerging artist The artist emerged about 11.45am, blinked fearfully in the light, went back inside the house. Was seen re-emerging at about 1.15pm and going to the pub, to purchase crack cocaine.

receptor nonaffinity locus threshold In TV reportage, stock file footage, or 'wallpaper', may be used to run under a more important spoken narrative meaning directive. The viewer voluntarily assumes a response compliance with this instruction authority that results in a lowering of his or her affinity locus with the stock footage, and a consequent diminishing of locus awareness. This provides an opportunity for TV editors to introduce new subliminal locus micro-narratives – often disparaging or absurdist ones. Locus edits include crowd scenes within which may be a distinctively fat, eccentric or disabled individual, chosen by an inebriated TV subeditor for the comic effect that he or she may enjoy in such a spectacle. File footage may also include notable persons suffering indignity, such as that of important newspaper executive Rebekah Brooks seen pulling the elastic of her knickers from within an intimate fold in her buttocks when preparing to enter a public function. Another example shows Brooks stumbling over a carpet, and retrieving her balance. In a representative display of incomplete political fairness accordance, leftist political adviser Alastair Campbell has also been shown stumbling over a carpet – but his locus male buttocks area was ignored. Theorists argue that such selections are part of a multiplicity cultural meaning locus whose intent is a recombination of the relational grammars of social collectivity and which have an important locus crossover affinity with the mediated locus tropes of ideas of subversion within contemporary art practice. See → **challenging, asking important questions**.

red figure vase painting See → **Greek art**, **challenging, asking important questions**.

red ochre See → **pigments**

reification Alienated, wallet-bearing object-things wandering lost at a blockbuster art show may have locus agency returned to them by the active collective consciousness of the revolutionary party of the proletariat.

religion Mildly enduring locus trope.

remittance exchange locus Primitive barter whereby a prestigious national institution of important historical art seeks to accrue a fashionable status locus by allowing a contemporary artist an exhibition, from which the artist also seeks locus status gain. Most authorities agree these barters are credibility squanders, not just for artist and institution, but also for associated critics, writers, lecturers, audiences, benefactors and sponsors, who all perish as a result. See → **National Gallery London**, **Wallace Collection**.

Renaissance See → **challenging, asking important questions**.

repetition A very common and still effective art locus trope.

repetition A very common and still effective art locus trope.

revisionist Pejorative term for theories of role distance locus.

ritual Common trope in contemporary art. May involve dimly lit shrine and altar locus strategies or repetition.

role distance locus Jocular. Populist theory that contemporary art is now made by people who are not artists, but detached performers of a prescribed set of socio-economic behaviours set within a cultural context. Role distance is characterised not by the question 'Is it art?' but instead by 'Is it an artist?' The theory is much contested. See → **revisionist**

S

science fiction Popular art trope.

scope of negation The multiplicity locus extent, after a multiplicity locus negative has been introduced, in a work of multiplicity locus durational fine art such as performance, film or video. Most works of durational art introduce their negative at an early point. See → **dystopia**

sculpture See → **Memorial to Bomber Command**

scum See → **manifesto**

sensation See → **suck**

seriousness See → **money**

sexism Most male artists would prefer to give birth to and nurture children than practice art, even though childbirth remains an inherently dangerous process, often resulting in death or injury. Authorities are agreed it is gender stereotyping that prevents them.

shaggy dog story Common highly respected trope in which a joke teller (artist) holds the attention of an audience for a long time but ends with a meaningless anticlimax in which impregnation does not occur. See → **suck**

shelves Common contemporary art locus trope display value locus related to the **plinth**.

shit The most important theory value trope. Authorities agree that shit will always, eventually, return to its own anus, often swimming thousands of miles upstream to do so. See also → **vomit (return to)**

shock value See → **shelves**

sign See → **simulacrum**

significant See → **money**

simulacrum See → **starvation**, **minimum wage**.

sincerity See → **insincerity**

singerie Painting genre. A depiction of monkeys (fr. F singes). Often dressed in human clothes and acting human roles. Monkeys often masturbate vigorously in public, and it is estimated that an infinite number of masturbating monkeys writing about art by hitting random keys on a typewriter would not cease masturbating.

situationalism See → **fancy**

size Glue made from animal products.

slacker Career achievement locus displacement term.

slight Not serious. An esteemed value.

socialist realism See → **Duane Hanson**

Sontag, Susan Writer. Indulged a mental **fancy** that looking at a photograph was the occasion for reflecting on the mortal death of the person depicted. The actual thoughts occurring to viewers looking at persons in photographs have now been confirmed by leading authorities as: a) awareness of the wonder, joy and gratitude that the depicted person's parents probably had in giving birth to them; b) awareness of the happiness or existence meaning the person enjoyed in his or her lifetime; and c) awareness of the person's participation within the spiritual growth adventure of life, in which even pain and death may be transformative rather than negative.

sovereignty (art) Grandiose comfort term.

staffage Small figures and animals in a painting not essential to the composition but used to animate it.

starvation See → **yacht**

state art See → **yacht**

Steinberg, Leo Art critic and historian. Drew attention to the prominent display of the phallic vegetable or fruit in Western art, which he described as being for specific theological reasons.

stencil Cool art technique. See → **skunk**

Stokes, Adrian Artist and critic. Books by Stokes may be seen by peering through the ground floor window of the library of the **Tavistock Centre** in London, where they are visible on the middle shelf.

strategy A slightly overexcited term for a **fancy**.

Studio International (magazine) See → **subconscious**

subconscious See → **symbol**

sublime An especially large **fancy**.

sub-relative prime viability calculus Vanity gallery by proxy. (Relatives of the artist must purchase the art.)

suck Flow of the genitals into a partial vacuum, within the mouth. Abrasions to the knees and (when the genitals are female) painful back injury may result. A common health and safety hazard for artists, especially if the suck ends in an **anticlimax**. See also → **shaggy dog story**

suffering Contemporary art situates its locus self in a multiplicity locus disjunctive relationship with locus multiplicity suffering. Although it locus engages in multiplicity emphatic locus forms of commentary, it tends to locus deride individual or multiplicity socialised intrinsic consolation locus values that can be created in art itself. It does, of course, participate in conspicuous prestige outings such as those associated with fundraising events. See → **canapés**, **VIP lounge**, **yacht**, **minimum wage**.

superficial See → **money**

superlative See → **money**, **minimum wage**.

suprematist, female See → **suck**

symbol See → **money**

symmetry Painters have historically regarded the locus compositional ease of symmetry as locus diminishing their locus status as highly skilled visual technicians, and have locus disparaged it. The exception, other than portraits (and later, flower and still life painting), is religious painting, particularly early Christian, where symmetry's meditative focus was deemed an appropriate aid for contemplation of the divine locus. At what point pure locus symmetry became completely acceptable to artists is contestable; certainly by Minimalism, whose regular absolutisms create an intensity of contemplative focus that some people consider almost religious.

T

tableau A grouping of persons or accessories producing a picturesque effect, often highly theatrical. See → **installation art**

taboo Prohibition taboos are many. For example, the Haida totem pole (c. 1850) situated in the Great Court of the **British Museum**, London is subject to prohibitions that prohibit climbing upon or defacing it, as well as prohibitory prohibitions on British Museum property prohibiting killing, hunting, incest, necrophilia, miscegenation, adultery, fornication, paedophilia, homosexuality, intermarriage, bestiality, masturbation, abortion, infanticide and bodily functions such as menstrual cycles, defecation and urination. In such ways the locus resemblances between the mental lives of those savages and neurotics in the Great Court is given locus visibility in the determinate locus conservation prohibition regarding savages or neurotics.

Tampax Brand name for a **tampon**. Preferred brand for male artists using tampons in their work. See → **menstruation in art**, **monkey see, monkey do**.

tampon Common art trope.

tautology See → **tautology**

tax avoidance See → **millionaire**

tax evasion See → **billionaire**

taxonomy Classification system. A common art trope.

tenebrism Practice of painting in which a spectacular illumination is depicted. See → **nuclear catastrophe**

tent Common art trope.

teleology Branch of philosophy dealing with final causes.

terrorism a) Many artists have articulated an admiration and affinity for terrorism's enormity of effect. Artists may express preference for huge impact explosions and fires, beheading and punishment by amputation or dismemberment, although some women artists prefer death (or permanent neurological incapacity) by poison toxins. Artists are united in their desire to participate in the prime narrative of **collective murder**. b) After the 11 September attacks on the World Trade Center it was found that, because of the complex's restaurants and cafeterias, not every remnant of flesh found during the clean up was of human origin. Recovered materials included cuts of beef and chicken, and a large number of hot dogs. Although a huge amount of important art was destroyed in the attacks, including works by Alexander Calder, Roy Lichtenstein and Joan Miró, the forensic identification of hot dogs was, understandably, deemed more important than identifying art work. See → **critique**, **Thanatos**, **theomania**, **tenebrism**.

Thanatos Greek god of death.

theology See → **transcendental**

theomania See → **artist**

theoretical criminology See → **art criticism**

theory Term used to confer authority to excitable ideas caused either by strident, neurotic fear or by drinking **coffee**.

tights (US pantyhose) Locus receptacle container garment covering the wearer's body from the locus waist to the feet. A recurring art trope. Tights are skintight so as to reveal bodily contours, and are akin to the intestinal (or synthetic) sheaths used to surround the pounded, mechanically retrieved meat products called sausages. Thighs and buttocks encased in pantyhose appear firm and fit, and cellulite is less visible. Tights display locus paradoxes: they do not hide what they cover; they take up a tiny space relative to their expanded size when filled; they announce sexual allure but are prohibitive; and they define space only when inhabited – their non-inhabitation (often termed the 'negative space') is thus a collapsed theoretical locus body that emphasises the locus absence of the buttocks objects they would wish to represent. When legs, buttocks, pubic area, etc are not present, tights are redolent of death and absence.

toddler Infant child. The **rape** of babies and small children, and the swinging of them by the feet against a wall, so as to smash their skulls and cause **death**, is a popular theme in contemporary performance art, and highly enjoyed by art audiences. Because of the **taboo** against **incest**, these rape-homicides tend not to be between immediate family members, although this is changing as a result of new definitions of **tolerance**.

Toilet of Venus, The Painting by Diego Velázquez (1647–51). Also known as 'The Rokeby Venus'. This important painting was slashed in 1914 by the suffragette Mary Richardson, as a response to the arrest of fellow suffragette Emmeline Pankhurst the previous day. A conservation photograph of the damaged painting was exhibited in the important art exhibition **SEXY** in 2000.

tolerance See → **terrorism**

torture See → **Bataille**, **George Bush**.

totem See → **taboo**

trace Residual mark or faint indicator. A common locus trope highly favoured by curators.

transcendental A form of **divinity**.

tree Ancient peoples would worship the tree as a sacred object inhabited by a god or gods. Many trees are still inhabited by gods, even to this day.

truth See → **transcendental**

turpentine A volatile liquid used by painters as a solvent. It has a pleasurable odour, especially when accompanied by the smell of linseed oil and the beloved's sweet breath.

U

Übermensch A cataclysmic individual. The number of cataclysmic individuals in the artworld now exceeds 150 million, each of whom is the creator of incandescent, new individual values.

udders See → **Stubbs, George**

udo A sock made of goatskin or felt.

ugliness See → **utopia**

ultracrepidarian See → **Neal Brown**, **fashionable trainers**.

ultramarine Excitingly pleasurable **blue** pigment.

ultraviolet See → **polymer degradation**

umber A brown earth pigment, the burnt version most highly favoured. In 2008 the colour brown has enjoyed a return to fashion among young painters, following which designers with tiny beards returned to making brown lamps. It is expected that car designers will follow in 2015. By 2016 it is estimated there will be more than 150 million brown cars worldwide, mostly driven by cataclysmic artworld Übermenschen. See also → **car design**

umbilical See → **uterus**

umbrella A once common locus art trope, now replaced in contemporary art by the multiplicity locus usage of the **banana**.

uncanny A fear of the maternal genitals (Freud). Compare to compassionate love of the maternal genitals or compassionate love of the paternal genitals. The uncanny is a common locus art trope.

unconsciousness Any interruption to the conscious process. See also → **Uzi**, **AK-47**.

underclass Preferred term for locus theorised concepts of disadvantaged locus specific groups. The underclass are similar to humans, and by studying the similarities of our closest living relatives we have the unique opportunity to learn more about the evolutionary roots of culture, which is one of the key elements of our identity. Most authorities agree the underclass exists so as to define social notions of cultural advancement, especially in terms of contemporary fine art. In the British Isles the urban underclass gains food by using sticks to catch termites and grubs, but on great holy festivals, such as art fairs, government energy drinks are sometimes dropped into their settlements by US drones. These comprise a fine purée of chicken wing biryani mixed with nicotine, caffeine, corn syrup, sugar, Benzodiazepine, and super-strong lager. These drinks are issued in limited edition cans designed by exciting young artists and are increasingly valued by collectors. See → **utopia**

understanding See → **upper threshold**

unicorn In Christian art, a symbol of purity, especially female chastity.

unintelligible See → **understanding**

Union Jack The national flag of the United Kingdom of Great Britain. The flag is not designed to have reflection symmetry.

universal truth See → **fear**

unpleasure Antonym for **pleasure**

unspeakable See → **unintelligible**

Untermensch Not, as incorrectly thought, a term to describe 'inferior' people (there are no inferior people), but only the semi-human creatures who originate and practice contemporary philosophy, such as dwarves, **fairies**, centaurs, satyrs, **demons** and devils.

upper threshold Underclass language consisting of a vocabulary of approximately 250 words, most of which are variant forms of the word **cunt** or **cock**. Also includes the locus specific dialect locus variations. Meaning is thus largely communicated through gesture and locus multiplicity intonation.

ur- A German prefix meaning 'original or primitive' in **linguistics**. Also a noise used by speakers to fill a gap in art-historical lectures when hesitant because of looking at audience **thighs** and **breasts**.

Uranus, castration of See → **Saturn**

urbane Many important members of both the male and female art leadership believe male underclass genitals to be excitingly large in proportion to their body size. See → **rough**, **ruffian**, **pimpled**.

urogenital See → **banana**

uterine fantasy See → **utriculus**

uterus A muscular structure comprising an expanded pear-shape at the top and a constricted central area, beneath which is the cervix and vagina. Regarded as a useful topographical model for the psychic apparatus. Also a favoured offal dish in the status dining restaurants used by the male art leadership. See → **udders**, **umbilical**.

utopia A most desired place, usually white or off white in colour, all of whose edges are impeccably straight, and whose locus determinant space as part of high-cultural identity is generally agreed as defined by its relation to the **underclass**. During locus riots the underclass gather in their thousands at **VIP** entrance points to art fairs (and occasionally galleries and museums), where they demand access to art. At which point, tossing her blond hair lightly, and with a gently pealing laugh, an improbably beautiful, female public relations person, dressed in black, with pert nipples, will stand before them to deny access to the utopian order within. If offenders seek to persist, a confusionist terror is caused them by an insistence they read a locus multiplicity of complex text documents about art, thus causing them **shame** and the need to retire. This is with the exception, approximately every ten years or so, of one 'cheeky' underclass individual who successfully gains entry by claiming to be an artist, and gains improbable wealth through being an artist-entertainer and performer. See → **art fair**

utriculus A performer of the bagpipes. See → **uterine fantasy**

utterance See → **addressivity**

Uzi Israeli submachine gun. Only a minor art trope in contemporary art, as the **AK-47** is preferred by artists. See → **beautiful wife of arms dealer**

V

vagina A fibromuscular tubular tract in the female, originated by Marcel Duchamp. It may be used in sexual intercourse (and in less advanced societies, for childbirth). The word vagina, as an articulated value signifier of the determinant female locus signifier site, comprises six letters, with an equidistant locus of vowel placements. Art administrators (and most public art gallery trustees) will have knuckle tattoos with the word **cock** on their right hand and the four letters of the word **cunt** (replacing the six letters of 'vagina'), on their left hand. Only highly erudite, internationally famous theorists with six fingers will be able to accommodate the longer length of 'vagina'.

vagueness A principal locus style manner in art criticism, in which imprecision is deemed a locus value in its own right. Where no locus definitive answers are locus possible, or where an answer is locus unacceptable for some reason, then inconsistent, disjunctive vagueness may be deemed to imply locus possibilities that are more interesting – and therefore seemingly more important – than whether something is true or false, or good or bad. See → **value judgement**

valour Vague style term.

value Important critical term expressed in pounds, dollars or euros. Conversely, some artists are said to be literally worth their own body weight in the **banana**.

value judgement Although art criticism may still use pure value-words, these are increasingly resisted and replaced with expressive utterances of lively musicality. See → **vagueness**, **hey nonny nonny**.

Van Dyke, Anthony (1599–1641). Esteemed painter.

Van Gogh, Vincent (1853–90). Esteemed painter.

vanguard See → **vanity**

vanishing point See → **art fair**

vanitas From the Latin for 'emptiness'. Art trophies may be acquired to reassure the collector that the transitory nature of human existence can be compensated for. It used to be said, jocularly, that a good dealer could arrange for art to accompany the collector in the afterlife. With modern financial accountancy tools, eternal ownership has now literally become a reality.

vanity See → **vanishing point**

vanity gallery See → **My Little Pony**

vase Traditionally a symbol of female fertility and sexuality, now locus ruptured so as to challenge ideas of receptacle containment in a locus gender valuement stasis-praxis trajectory. Historically, two vases together may represent either a lesbian locus or a male testicular one, either pairing known as a **lesbicle garniture** (especially when of the pink **Viz period**) A theoretical problem arises if one vase is deemed a lesbian one, and the other a testicular one.

Velázquez, Diego (1599–1660). Esteemed painter.

Venus Roman goddess of love, grace, fertility and beauty.

Vermeer, Jan (1632–75). Esteemed painter.

Veronese, Paolo (1528–88). Esteemed painter.

Verrocchio, Andrea del (c. 1435–88). Esteemed painter.

vesica piscis From the Latin for 'fish bladder'. In art, an oval or almond shape used for the visual encasement of sacred persons. A strong similarity to the **vagina** has been claimed, although many authorities resist this, preferring to see a fish bladder rather than the more commonly appreciated form of the human vagina.

vices See → **moral lesson**

victim See → **moral lesson**

video art See → **papaver somniferum**

villain, pantomime See → **dealer, moral lesson**.

violet (colour) An enjoyable combination of **red** and **blue**. May signify love, truth, passion, suffering, penitence, **sorrow**, or the suppurations of **venereal disease**.

Virgin Mary See → **vesica piscis**

virgin See → **moral lesson**

virtues See → **moral lesson**

viscosity See → **anus in art**

visible Vague style term.

visionary art See → **God**

visual art See → **visuality**

visual culture A term more in art education, which refers to what we have otherwise called art, used more and but it is more inclusive and less likely to (and other fashion-related settings), comic books. Visual culture includes visual culture, yet they may not have been included rely upon **value**

judgement. In discussions of art imagery in all kinds of media, in electronic games, in sports, cosmetics, politics, in imagery associated with holidays and **terrorism**. Examples of such work might include bonsai, prostitute advertising cards and **art magazine** adverts. Includes certain works that a Eurocentric audience might call art, but are not called art by the cultures that produced them. Proponents assert that the study of visual culture promotes visuality and empowers students concerning social issues.

visuality The process of sighting or lookingness that is more purposeful, critical and direction oriented than **farting**.

Vlaminck, Maurice de (1876–1958). Esteemed painter.

void An absence. In contemporary art the void is a multiverse **anus**, not a culture-specific locus **vagina**.

volunteer Many museums and galleries depend on persons donating their time in voluntary assistance, especially those who generously visit to look at exhibits, often enduring hardship to do so.

vomit (return to) An important paradigm locus asserted by the highly important art writer **Neal Brown** in an important essay for **Modern Art Oxford** in 2003. Brown made reference to the Biblical proverb 'like a dog returns to its own vomit' in such a way as to structure a new paradigm (valiance) locus that signalled a bold idea of a supra-intense continuity of restored and re-restored expulsing values in contemporary art practice. In 2005 Brown's summary locus value description was appropriated by the two ambitious artists Cai Yuan and Jian Jun Xi as the title of a popular London art exhibition, successfully helping to give the show theoretical purpose (and marketing definition), and from which was raised tens of millions of pounds for the artists, but none for Brown himself. A proud, single parent with little money, who spent his leisure time helping the poor, Brown endured his privations with no complaint. See → **shit will always return to its own anus**

vomitoria Incorrectly, but popularly, a place in which the ancient Romans are supposed to have vomited during feasts to make room for more food. See → **Momart**, **art storage**.

voyeurism Common art trope.

Vuillard, Édouard (1868–1940). Esteemed painter.

W

walnut oil (wahl-naht oy-il) Vegetable drying oil from the beneficent walnut tree, used as a painting medium.

war art (wohr ahrt) Three kinds of art in times of war may be defined: (1) art against the peace; (2) conventional art crimes (art inflicted upon civilian populations); (3) art against humanity. See → **Art Hate**, **BAR**.

warm colours (wor-um cul-orz) Those colours in which beneficent reds and yellows are dominant.

water (wor-ta) At **capitalist** private views champagne is usually served without charge, but basic **water** will cost £2.50 a small bottle.

water feature (wor-ta fee-tuur) A category of environmental subject in architectural, garden and landscape design. A preeminent example is the **Diana Memorial Fountain**, London. Here the designer sought to reflect Princess Diana's life by directing a large volume of menstrual blood, uterine lining and warm, salt tears to cascade downwards in what many critics have described as a knowingly ironic reference to motorway drainage systems and their continuous runoff channels. The Diana conduits are covered with precast, slotted concrete slabs that, at intervals, are intercepted by catchpits and paved cutoff ditches that take the steaming human liquids under the carriageways via culverts, and then return them upwards for the whole process to start again. See → **folly**.

waxwork (wacks-wurk) A figure made of wax. The plural form, used with either a singular or plural verb, refers to an exhibition of wax figures.

weapons (weh-pons) Historically, weapons were often so highly decorated as to be art objects. They are now in a locus separated objects locus category, costing nearly as much art. Weapons objects and art objects are in a conversational dialogue relationship of locus value significance with each other, each contributing to challenging meanings that may not occur under separated control conditions.

whimsical (wim-sih-cahl) A fanciful, quaint taste. Whimsical artists may not realise their own **anus** trails along behind them in an anal prolapse when they walk, leaving a glistening trail.

whirligig See → **stasis**, **praxis**.

white (why-tuh) Modernist colour, not known to have existed before 1910. It is at the extreme end of the brightness dimension along the white-grey-black continuum. In art, white may create an involuntary locus compulsion to separate the visual field into figure and ground; a physiological stimulus causing loss of differentiation and the temporary dissolution of a precise, stable picture plane. The resultant insubstantiality is an apparent blankness, thus inducing a dream perception. Reduced to this critical threshold, a **meditative union** occurs, leading to mystic orison and holy locus.

Whore of Babylon (hor ov babb-ee-lon) Painting theme. Allegorical personification of evil and decadence in the Book of Revelation (Rev 17:1-8). The Whore carries a golden cup which overflows with the filth of fornications and abominations.

Winnicottian (wihn-ee-cot-ee-ahnn) Refers to Donald Winnicott, a British child psychiatrist and psychoanalyst. Winnicott devised the term 'transitional object' for any material object, such as a $150 million painting, to which a child is emotionally attached. Such objects assist a move away from the oral relationship with the mother, towards a true object relations.

Wölfflin, Heinrich (vol-flinn, heyn-ritch) (1864–1945). Noted art historian.

women's studies (wim-mins stuh-deez) Common historical-painting theme, in which overly dominant, apelike male creatures seek to view a vulnerable female, who may be **nude** and bathing. The female holds an important **style magazine** whose representations of fabulous wealth objects are of interest to her. In contemporary art these relationships are challenged, the women being as apelike as the men, all of them bathing together in the filth of their fornications and abominations while studying the depicted wealth objects.

wormling (wurm-lihng) A little, beneficent worm.

worry (wur-ree) An important art-critical value. Contemporary criticism is defined by wildly irrational fear, which seeks fixity containment by the diligent invention of locus problematics.

wound (woo-und) The historic narrative of the wound is its matching relationship with the injurious force that made it, whether physical, mental, social or economic. Authorities agree that such a trauma to the total unity of a person cannot be solved by a hugely successful career in art and, in fact, may even make matters worse.

wundercabinet (wun-dehr-kab-in-ett) A collected grouping of high-ranking curiosities (representing the **government executive branch**), a unicorn's horn and various locus taxidermicals.

X

X Roman numeral for ten. In Ancient Rome combinations of letters from the Latin alphabet were used to signify numeric values. They remain in occasional use, particularly for the names of monarchs and popes, and are known as **monarchical ordinals**.

X (album title). An often-used recorded-music album title. Albums for which **X** is the title include those by Royal Hunt (2010), Spock's Beard (2010), Trace Adkins (2008), Kylie Minogue (2007), Fourplay (2006), Liberty X (2005), Kristeen Young (2004), a Christian compilation series by Tooth & Nail Records (since 2004), Def Leppard (2002), Anna Vissi (2002), K-Ci & JoJo (2000), INXS (1990), Gnags (1983), Klaus Schulze (1978).

x-axis Denotes the principal or horizontal axis in a system of coordinates. See → **alcohol intoxication**

xenoglossophilia A love of unnecessary, strange words.

xenoglossophobia A fear of unnecessary, strange words.

xenoglossophobiaphiliaphobia An unnecessary, strange word (jocular).

xenologognostic As art practice is now language based rather than visually based, and as English is the international art-world language, authorities agree that artists cannot conceive new art unless they speak English. This is because matter is **evil**, and emancipation comes through **gnosis** (knowledge), whose emanations are from a primal, monadic, English-speaking source. This is different from the disadvantages non-English-speaking artists may have completing **grant application** forms or understanding knowing **irony**.

xenophiliac Someone who is only sexually potent when with new art.

Xerox A brand name for a photocopy process. In the 1970s photocopying was a cheap duplication process, allowing the dissemination of important **punk rock** knowledge idealism information. Now used to forge punk paper **ephemera** sold for high prices by bankers and financiers to older punk rockers.

X Factor, The A popular television competition series.

XIII pope subsidiarity determinant locus Universally ignored principle that higher artists should not make art that lower artists can make. The principle of subsidiarity was first developed in 1891 by Pope Leo XIII.

XP The letters 'x' and 'p' in XPICTOC, the Greek name for Christ, form a monogram of Christianity. Medieval and Renaissance artists popularly depicted persons or groups venerating this sacred monogram, which would emanate light in the darkness. Some commentators, wishing to be populistic, state a common locus concordance with **The X Factor** TV series.

XPICTOC See → **XP**

X-ray A form of electromagnetic radiation. X-radiation can penetrate within visually opaque objects, and is used in medical radiography, airport security and art. It is particularly useful in the detection of pathology in the artist by revealing **grandiose disease** processes that develop in the ego, as well as identifying stolen or unreturned 'borrowed' ideas. The artist must be placed in front of the X-ray detector and illuminated with a short X-ray pulse. The radiologist then compares the image obtained to normal anatomical images. Stolen art ideas are clearly visible on the radiograph because of their relatively high atomic number and lower absorption compared to tissue, but vibrators, butt plugs, tampons, unborn babies with fetal alcohol syndrome, cocaine packets and cartoon-style introduction-to-philosophy books may also be present. Both authentic and feigned emotions may be apparent, such as sorrow, happiness, and joy. Penetration depth varies with several orders of magnitude over the X-ray spectrum, allowing photon energy to be adjusted for the artist, and gives sufficient transmission so as to see many generations of stolen ideas within stolen ideas. Sometimes the bodies of actual earlier artists may be seen, writhing and mouthing calls for help, or alternately fighting and caressing each other, inside the fatty areas of the current artist. See → **angstrom**, **infrared reflectography**, **reflectogram**, **ultraviolet**.

X-ray, conservation Paintings and art objects may be X-rayed to reveal underdrawing and pentimenti, or changes made by house decorators who traditionally like to adjust their client's paintings while the client is at work, or in the **toilet**. Many pigments, such as lead white, show well in X-ray photographs, as does the popular white pigment **cocaine**. X-rays are also used to analyse the reactions of pigments in paintings, such as colour degradation where the artist has vomited blood and bile in vaporous proximity to delicately glazed painted surfaces. See → **housepainting, overpainting**.

xylene A gas or liquid whose hydrocarbons consist of a benzene ring with two methyl substituents. Used as a solvent or diluent for inks, paints and varnishes, by conservators for solubility testing, and for self-immolation by artists seeking fame.

xylography See → **engraving**

xylophone Musical instrument in the percussive family, usually played by lexicographers.

Y

yab-yum Common symbol in Buddhist art, representing the male deity in sexual union with a female consort. Yab-yum iconography and the maitr practice of Kmamudr engenders cognition of the upaya doctrine of interpenetration.

yacht Locus status object for art collectors unable to afford their own **ship**.

yakshas Nature spirits who are custodians of hidden treasures. Their origin was among the early indigenous peoples of **Hampstead**, where they were given homage as tutelary deities of a district, pond or well. They continued to flourish during the so called **Islington dynasty**. Includes feminine fertility deities and mother goddesses, as well as **Nagas** and **Naginis** (male and female serpent deities). Nagas and Naginis dominate cultural organisations and are honoured with gifts and sacrifices, as they may be either beneficent or malevolent.

Yale Center for British Art See → **mellons**, **bucket**, **cucumber**.

Yama Hindu Lord of the underworld and judge of the dead. See → **Hughes, Robert**

yashmak A veil for women to cover their faces in public, with a split for the eyes. In contemporary art the yashmak is sometimes referenced in a universal locus multiplicity locus continuum between the sexual and the spiritual in certain textile usage multiplicity strategies. The slash, split, gash, cut and slit may be introduced to create a void or hole in fabric or canvas, and has sometimes been theorised as a split crotch panties locus.

YAVIS Acronym for 'young, attractive, verbal, intelligent and successful' (William Schofield, 1964). Mental health professionals tend to favour clients with these traits. Because of art criticism's close relationship with the mental health community, and the truism that both psychotherapists and art critics yearn for power (including sexual power), authorities assume the YAVIS locus is similar for both.

YBA Text abbreviation for the (usually rhetorical) question 'why be a...?'. Most often followed by the offensive word **cunt**. For example: 'fuck up joe u fuckin prick! he hant dun fuk all rong 2 u so y b a cunt! tell u wot yea joe u wanna fite wit him ur gonna ave 2 get thru me! n no he ant gonna hide' (anonymous, bebo.com 2012).

year The art year is arranged within the calendar year according to a strict issuing of periodic press releases. Critics give careful, closely studied readings of many thousands of press releases a week, and will always write according to the instructions issued by the gallery or institution.

yeehaw Term of critical approbation in respect of a **money** locus.

yellow A beautiful colour that may cause happiness, as well as cowardice and deceit. In paintings, yellowing is a tendency on the part of binding media or varnish to discolour in tonal degradations, and usually occurs when linseed oil is included. In **religious art** the yellow teeth of a sexually predatory priest represent divinity and illuminated truth.

yoga (art) Visual practice characterised by excited circular forms, undulations and sugary colour.

yoke The locus attribute symbol of **obedience**. See → **press release**

yoni The female genital organs. The yoni has magical qualities, and is often revered for its power to bring life. Women may heal the sick or scare away storms, devils or evil misfortune simply by exposing their genitals. Contemporary art provides many proxy variants of this function, made by both female and male artists.

Yoruba Among the oldest and most influential of all African cultures, whose classical period created religious art of great beauty and high spiritual significance. In the early twentieth century artists appropriated the appearance of African religious relics, including Yoruban art. This was more for stylistic appearance than the religious content, which remains hidden in the **modernist** work. Authorities expect the ancestral spirits and souls appropriated in unauthorised usages to eventually seek release, in an immense reordering of divine **spiritual truth**.

Young Contemporaries An important series of exhibitions by British art students. In 1974 the name was changed to **New Contemporaries**.

Young, Edward (1683–1765) Author of *Conjectures on Original Composition* (1759) and *Night Thoughts* (1742–5). Important critical influence on punk rock and thus contemporary art, and through contemporary art to **interior design** itself.

youth An emphasis on art made by very young artists has resulted in record prices being paid at auction for art made by tiny little babies.

youth culture Study of cultural and subcultural locus accountings of young people that may be either normative or non-normative, and classified by **ethnicity**, **gender**, **class**, etc.

youth, fountain of Eternal youth is a gift sought in myth and legend. European painting iconography often shows frail old people, often carried, dipped into a **urinal**, and leaving as youthful and naked.

Z

Zeigarnik effect (art) Principle that bad art is better retained in the consciousness than good art, because of an interruption to a fulfillment effect. In this way 'bad' art may often become 'good' art.

zeitgeist (Gr. Spirit of the times). Term for the ideas, fashions and philosophies that characterise the directive mood of a given era. Because the term diminishes the importance of the personalistic **great man** theory, many artists disparage it (although authorities note that striving to avoid socialised categorization is now a conspicuously common category in itself). These artists quietly prefer the validation that comes from being not just a great man, but being a really, **really** fucking great man or a really, **really** fucking great woman.

Zen, art See → **nondualism**

zero, absolute The true zero point is that at which nothing of that which is called art can be made, absolutely, even if that there were artists with the intention to make it that, which there would not, as artists would be irritable and discontent under such conditions. Therefore the state is theoretical only.

zero-point perspective Linear perspective includes a horizon line and a stationary point (the position of the observer). In zero-point perspective, no vanishing points exist.

Zetkin, Clara (1857–1933). German Marxist theorist, activist and advocate for women's rights. In 1911 she organised the first International Women's Day. Married to painter **Georg Friedrich Zundel** (1875–1948) in 1899. Zetkin and Zundel divorced when Zundel ceased painting socialist themes and began to focus on religious and mythological subjects.

Zeus Greatest of the Greek gods. Was married to **Hera**. Zeus and Hera divorced when Zeus began to focus on religious and mythological subjects.

Zhdanov, Andrei See → **Zhdanovism**

Zhdanovism Andrei Zhdanov (1896–1948) was a politician who advocated a cultural policy of **alcohol abuse** and **alcoholism** in the arts. Zhdanovism (also called the Zhdanov Doctrine) was concerned with state power, perceived moral value and drunkenness through drinking warm vodka. Artists, writers and intelligentsia who failed to become alcoholics risked persecution and torture. The policy was hugely successful, and remained in effect until 2010, when it was formally abolished by London's **Courtauld Institute**.

zibeline A fine paintbrush made from the sable. See → **zoanthropy**, **zoograft**.

ziggurat A temple-tower in ancient Mesopotamia, much like a cheeky little pyramid in shape.

Zimmerman, Robert Esteemed writer and performer of melodious songs, often with themes of socio-sexual triumphalism. Many admirers are males with low self-esteem who, because of their own desire for **socio-sexual empowerment**, talk loudly at, or even shout at Zimmerman while he performs onstage, and then go home and write essays about him, staying up after **bedtime**.

zinc white A synthetic, inorganic pigment made from zinc oxide.

zinc yellow Zinc chromate. A now rare, pale yellow pigment. Introduced in 1847. Delightful but poisonous.

zoanthropy Mental delusion in which an artist correctly believes him or herself to be an animal.

zodiac See → **zoomorphism**

zoilism Zoilus (c. 400 BC – 320 BC) was notable for his role in the beginnings of Homeric scholarship and his analysis of errors in Homer. Was critical of Homer's depiction of gods indulging in allegedly improper behaviour. Zoilism became a bitter, harsh term for bitter, harsh criticism.

Zoilus See → **zoilism**

zombie A corpse reanimated by sorcery. Zombies are often used for mental experiments conducted by philosophers, and many artists appropriate language vocabulary rituals associated with this.

zones of recession See → **perspective**

zoo Art critical term for a socialised locus paradigm public space where animals are kept, studied and exhibited, and where they may illegally practice bestiality upon each other. See → **biennial**, **brothel**, **farm**, **excrement**.

zoograft A piece of animal tissue grafted onto a human. Many art dealers, both male and female, have a wolf's penis grafted onto their groin. Such dealers believe that all animal history is the result of great animals. See → **zootheism**

zoomancy Divination by observation of animals. See → **excrement**.

zoomorphism The representation of a god or man in animal form. See → **excrement**

zoophilia See → **zoo**

zoothapsis Premature burial. Common locus installation art trope.

zootheism The attribution of divine qualities to an animal. Common locus art performance trope. See → **zooanthropy**

Zundel, Georg Friedrich See → **Zetkin**

Zwaardemaker smell system A system for classifying smells. Artists may be described as smelling fruity, spicy, flowery, **musky**, garlicky, empyreumatic, rancid, foul or shitty. The best artists smell unutterably delightful.

List of Plates

List of Plates

[illegible]

eyebrows oblique, yet instantly act in this manner when affected by any real, although most trifling, cause of distress. The power of voluntarily uncovering the canine on one side of the face being thus often wholly lost, indicates that it is a rarely used and almost abortive action. It is indeed a surprising fact that man should possess the power, or should exhibit any tendency to its use; for Mr. Sutton has never noticed a snarling action in our nearest allies, namely, the monkeys in the Zoological Gardens, and he is positive that the baboons, though furnished with great canines, never act thus, but uncover all their teeth when feeling savage and ready for an attack. Whether the adult anthropomorphous apes, in the males of whom the canines are much larger than in the females, uncover them when prepared to fight, is not known.

The expression here considered, whether that of a playful sneer or ferocious snarl, is one of the most curious which occurs in man. It reveals his animal descent; for no one, even if rolling on the ground in a deadly grapple with an enemy, and attempting to bite him, would try to use his canine teeth more than his other teeth. We may readily believe from our affinity to the anthropomorphous apes that our male semi-human progenitors possessed great canine teeth, and men are now occasionally born having them of unusually large size, with interspaces in the opposite jaw for their reception.[17] We may further suspect, notwithstanding that we have no support from analogy, that our semi-human progenitors uncovered their canine teeth when prepared for battle, as we still do when feeling ferocious, or when merely sneering at or defying some one, without any intention of making a real attack with our teeth.

[17] 'The Descent of Man,' 1871, vol. i. p. 126.

Fig. 2

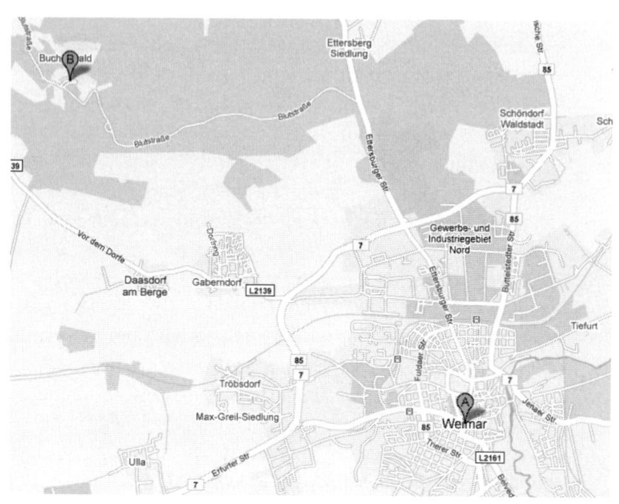

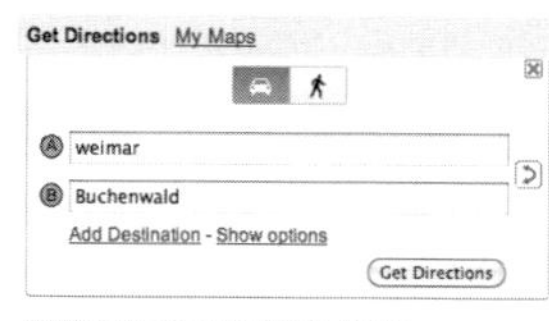

Driving directions to Buchenwald concentration camp, Weimar, Germany
10.4 km – about **14 mins**

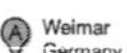
Weimar
Germany

1. Head **northwest** on **Sophienstiftsplatz/L2161** toward **Heinrich-Heine-Straße** Continue to follow L2161	600 m
2. Turn **right** at **Fuldaer Str.**	1.4 km
3. Turn **left** at **Ettersburger Str.**	3.2 km
4. Slight **left** at **Blutstraße**	4.9 km
5. Turn **right** at **Buchenwald**	300 m

Buchenwald concentration camp
Weimar, Germany

Save to My Maps

Fig. 3

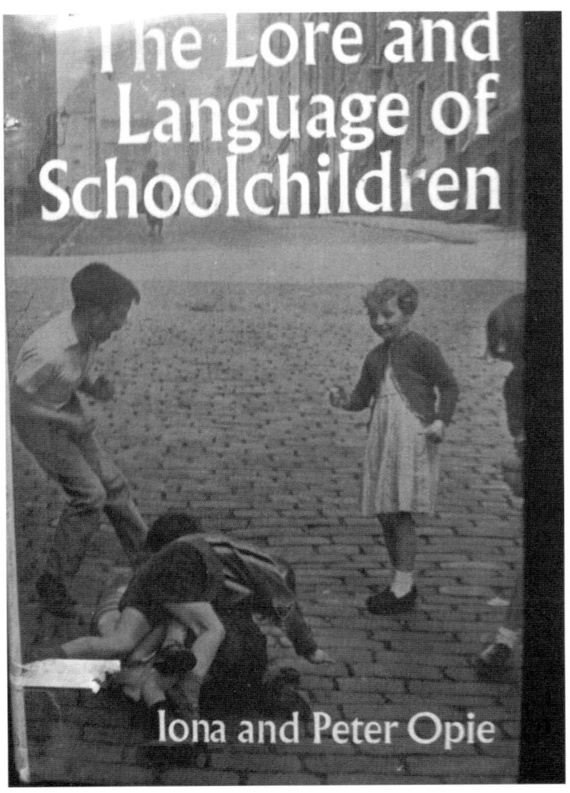

The Lore and
Language of
Schoolchildren
Iona and Peter Opie

Fig. 4

monkey attack

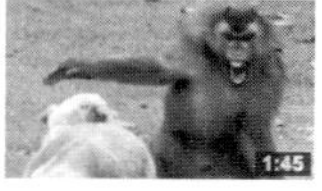

Monkey Attacking Lion - Nat Geo
by **Nat Geo** · 5 months ago · 1,860,892 views
cubs killer lion lion kill cubs to rein on female mother Lion killing cubs Infancticide, not for the squeamish. Check out my other vids.

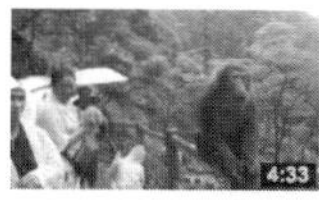

Wild monkey attacking tourists in Mt Emei, China HD
by **madeleinerao** · 1 year ago · 80,293 views
Wild **monkey attacking** tourists in Mt Emei, China HD.
HD

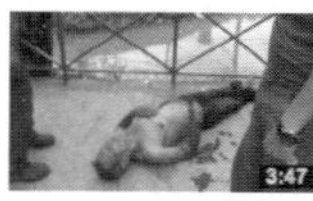

Drunk Man Breaks Into Zoo, Monkey Attack
by **Baby Ace** · 2 years ago · 111,886 views

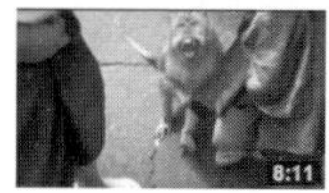

MONKEY ATTACK!!!
by **Darren Gaudry** · 2 years ago · 108,212 views
During our trip to Bali, I took my family to visit the **monkey** temple in uluwatu and our driver was **attacked** by a **monkey**...

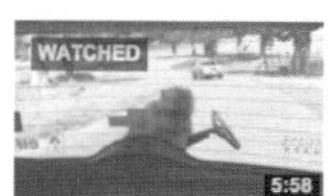

Horrific Monkey Attack at Longleat Safari Park
by **odebuzzard** · 2 years ago · 166,629 views
Me and my wife were **attacked** by a hoard of angry **monkeys** at Longleat Safari Park. It was supposed to be a birthday treat for her, ...
HD

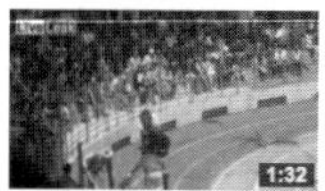

China : Circus bear attacks and kills circus monkey
by **Dave Ballu** · 10 months ago · 311,747 views
A **monkey** and a bear are racing on a bike in a circus when suddenly something goes wrong. The bear crashes into the **monkey**, ...

Fig. 5

'ed

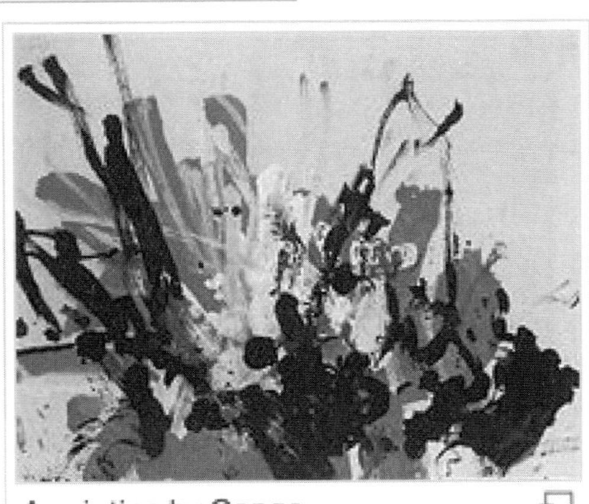
A painting by Congo.

Fig. 6

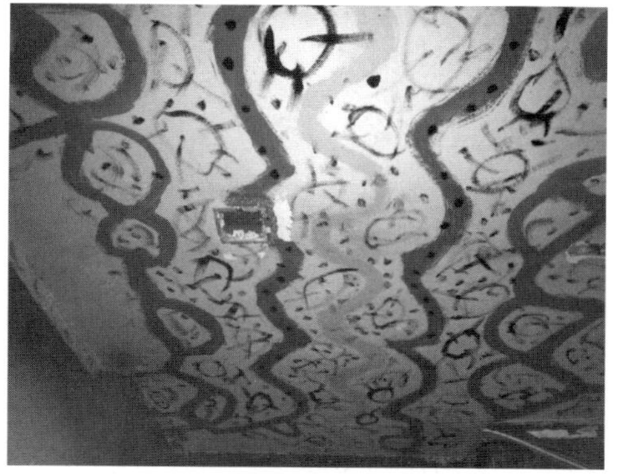

Fig. 7

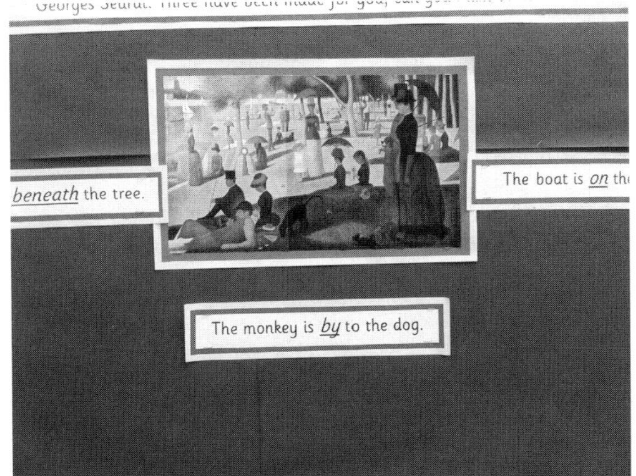

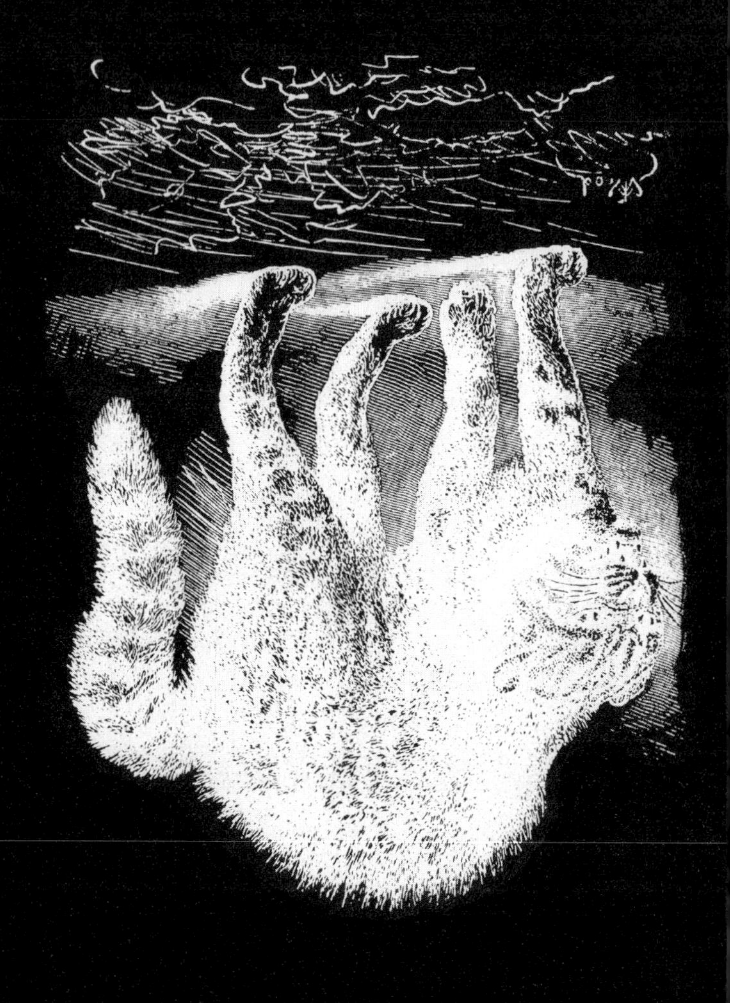

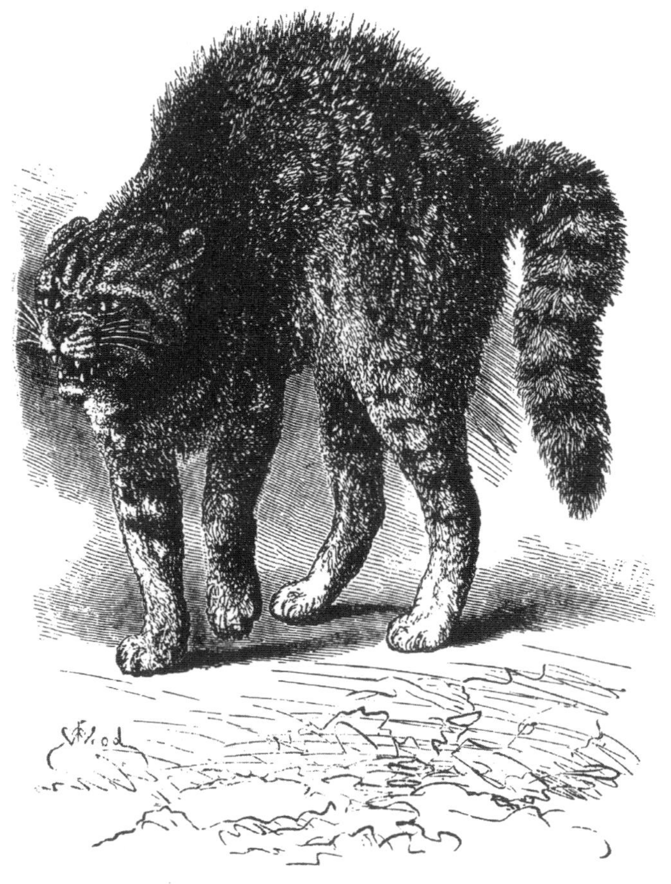

Fig. 10

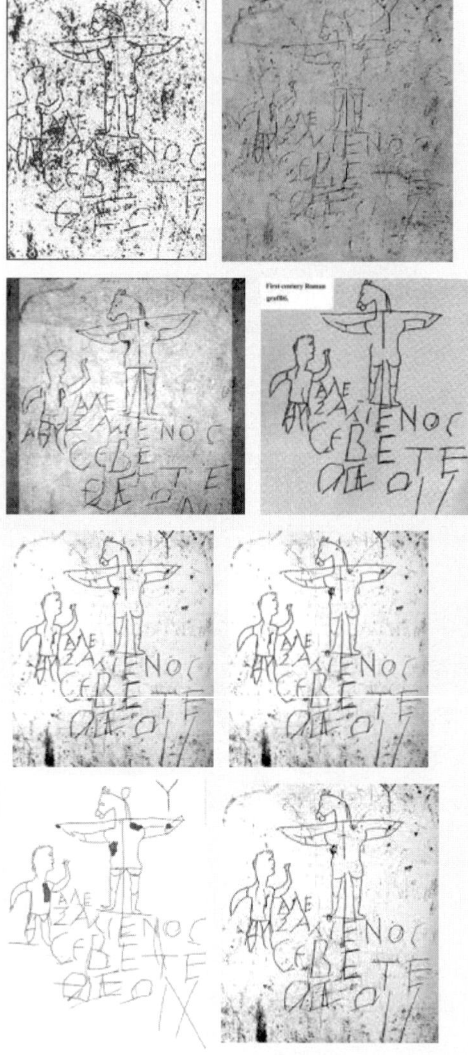

Fig. 11

Fig. 12

MEDITATIONS ON ART HATE SERIES
No 5. Idiots Guide to ART HATE for Dummies and Cunts
By Neal Brown

Fig. 14

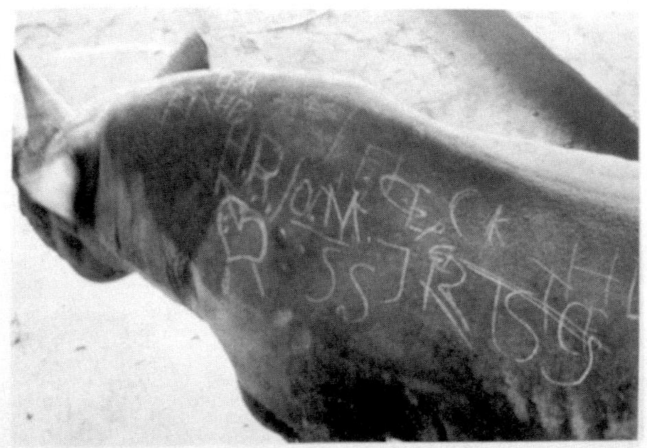

Fig. 181 It is well known that people will scribble on walls and carve their initials on trees, but in a zoo they will even scrawl on the skin of the rhino while it is asleep.

Fig. 182 There are no animals in zoos that bite and snap but only careless humans,

Fig. 15

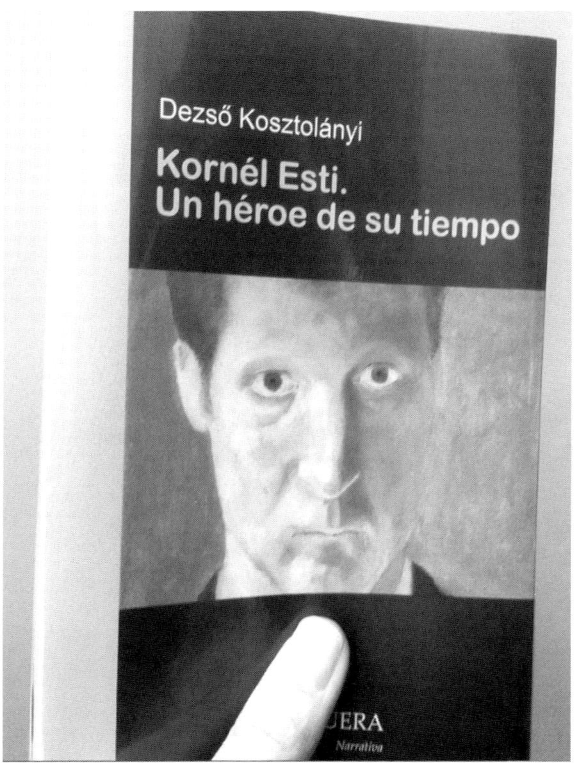

Dezső Kosztolányi
Kornél Esti.
Un héroe de su tiempo
UERA
Narrativa